The
VEGAN
IMPERATIVE

The
VEGAN
IMPERATIVE

Why We Must Give Up Meat
and Why We Don't

David Blatte

Pythagorean
Publishing

Contents

Introduction   *i*

Part One: Why Vegan?

Chapter 1: The Moral Imperative   3

Chapter 2: The Environmental Imperative   27

Chapter 3: The Health Imperative   45

Chapter 4: Speciesism   61

Chapter 5: Animal Law   79

Part Two: Why Not Vegan?

Part Two Introduction   *96*

Chapter 6: Cognitive Dissonance   97

Chapter 7: Reducing the Tension   111

Chapter 8: More Food for Thought   155

Chapter 9: Social Animals   185

Chapter 10: Making the Transition   195

Notes   *209*

Acknowledgments   *223*

Bibliography   *225*

Index   *235*

Introduction

A few years ago, my friend Mike said something that stuck in my mind. In the 20 years we've known each other, he's heard all the reasons for going vegan. One day, out of the blue, he made a confession. "Dave, I've been listening to you talk about vegetarianism and veganism for a long time now, and I have to tell you something: you're right." He paused. I waited for the inevitable. "… but I'm still going to eat meat!"

Veganism is undergoing a historic transformation. When I went vegetarian in 1977, it was weird, strange, eccentric. When I turned vegan 11 years later, it was unheard of. When I was executive director of Vegan Action in 2000 and established the "certified vegan" logo, it catered to a small, niche population. When I started an animal law practice in 2001, it remained an obscure field of law.

Everything has changed. Veganism has arrived. Vegan restaurants are everywhere, vegan options at other restaurants are standard, and even such carnivorous establishments as Burger King have joined the parade. Veganism permeates pop culture — everyone knows what it is, and the number of public personalities identifying as vegan grows daily. Animal law classes are commonplace at law schools.

But the conundrum remains. Good, caring people like Mike continue to eat meat and animal products. Despite the moral, environmental, and health implications of a nonvegan diet, veganism remains a minority choice. People dabble but don't commit. They praise its virtues but fail to embrace them. For most of my life, the question posed was: Why vegan? The question today is: Why *not* vegan? Faced with overwhelming reasons to change, why do kindhearted people—people like you—continue to eat animals and their products?

This book is the culmination of over forty years thinking about these questions. Divided into two parts, it begins with a comprehensive overview of the three main reasons people go vegan—morality, environment, and health. Each is compelling in its own right, and together with an exposition of speciesism they form a powerful, persuasive imperative. The chapter on animal law walks you through six real cases, offering a rare and illuminating behind-the-scenes look at this emergent legal field.

It's tempting to reduce the reasons people are not vegan to the simple statement "I like meat." This is certainly a big factor, but it's the beginning rather than end of the story. A more complete understanding involves topics like social norms, personality traits, and the phenomenon of cognitive dissonance. Part two looks at these and the broad range of psychological and cultural influences underpinning our decision to eat or not eat meat.

The narrative is presented through a combination of storytelling and more rigorous analysis. In addition to my perspective as a longtime vegan advocate, you'll be introduced to a number of people—meat-eaters, vegetarians, and vegans—who shared their personal stories with me and whose candid perspectives are interspersed throughout. They are actual people; some I knew already and others I met for the first time. I also circulated a brief online survey, and you'll hear from many of the respondents. These subjective viewpoints are complemented by extensive reference to a body of scientific research.

If you are not familiar with veganism, many of the ideas in this book will be novel for you. Meat-eating is surprisingly complex, implicating philosophy, psychology, sociology, anthropology, environment, health, and an assortment of unique considerations. Vegans too will discover new ways of thinking, and both vegans and nonvegans will see familiar concepts in a different light.

I still remember how difficult the decision to go vegetarian and then vegan was. It felt like I was giving up so much, that my life was changing irreversibly. It was scary, and I really didn't want to do it. Once I took the leap, it didn't take long for that feeling to vanish. Now I'm grateful for those decisions and wouldn't change a thing, except to have done it sooner. With easy access to healthy, tasty vegan food, going vegan is certainly easier today than it was 40 years ago, but it is a big step, nonetheless. For the animals, the earth, and your health, it's a step worth taking.

Part One:

Why Vegan?

Chapter 1:

The Moral Imperative

When I was twelve, I went on a road trip with my parents to Florida over winter vacation. On a seemingly uneventful day when we planned to visit a former student of my father, I woke up sick. He went alone, leaving my mother to nurse me back to health.

When I went to sleep that night, he had still not returned. The next thing I remember is being woken by a loud knock on the door. It was the police. They had devastating news. My father had been killed in a car accident.

The following weeks are largely a blur, but some images remain vivid in my mind. My sister and other relatives huddled in one big amorphous mass sobbing its way through the airport. The miles-long funeral procession—he was popular. Standing next to my aunt as they lowered the coffin into the ground on a clear, frigid December day. Perhaps portentously, I recall the feel of her fur coat as it rubbed against the back of my hand.

One memory stands out above the rest. For what seemed like weeks, if not months, I lay alone in my bed, the sound of my mother's sobs reverberating through my body as they resonated throughout the house. Even when she wasn't wailing, I could hear her relentless crying through the wafer-thin wall that separated our bedrooms. It was a singular, horrible time, forever etched in my consciousness.

This event, as tragedy does, changed the trajectory of my life. I sometimes wonder how different my path would have been if not for that fateful night. Is there a direct line from the accident to my becoming vegan, or was it always inevitable? It's impossible to know, of course. What I do know is that life went on.

Why Vegetarian?

At first, I was overwhelmed by suffering—the manifest grief of my mother, the quiet sorrow of my sister (like me, alone in her bedroom struggling to process her pain), and my own sadness, the loss of a beloved father compounded by the audible agony surrounding me. As time went on, my pain naturally diminished, and I started to turn outward again. I did so with a new perspective.

My house was in a wooded suburb of New York City. The giant window in the family room looked out into a forested backyard with not a single manmade structure in sight. Immersed in nature, my attention was drawn to the creatures that shared my environment. Through that glass I watched with curiosity and fascination as they busily attended to their lives. As I did, I was struck by a realization. Like me, my mother, and my sister, *they too suffered*. Like us, they avoided pain. When injured, they showed distress.

It was everywhere. A deer hit by a car, lying crippled and bewildered by the side of the road. A squirrel or raccoon with an open wound, unable to heal itself. A bird shivering in the snow. Even the insects seemed to suffer. A moth too close to a hot light bulb struggling to escape, fluttering its wings wildly until succumbing to its fate. A spider missing a leg, limping helplessly along.

This insight pierced me to the core. I was not alone in my suffering. We are not alone in our suffering. It does not belong to humans. Suffering is the common bond that unites all creatures, great and small. No one is immune. Though I couldn't know how animals experienced their suffering, that they suffered was undeniable.

Something else was equally apparent: animals fear death. For them it's not conceptual. With some possible exceptions, they aren't cursed with the awareness that someday they are going to die, the knowledge responsible for so much human existential angst. But when death is imminent, they sense it. And like us, they avoid it at all costs. Their will to live is just as strong as ours.

These realizations touched me deeply, and as I gazed out into their universe a strange feeling arose in me—*compassion*. Just as I knew the pain of my own suffering, my heart ached for the animals. It didn't matter that they were not human. Their suffering was just as real for them as mine was for me, and I shared it.

*

Despite this new perspective, I did not become vegetarian. My attention was drawn instead to the burgeoning anti-fur movement, which was making national headlines and nightly newscasts. I didn't approve of tactics like throwing red dye on fur coats, but I shared the outrage. Fur was barbaric and heartless. As a practical matter, there wasn't much a kid living in the suburbs could do about it. There was no outlet for my emerging activism. But a seed had been sown.

It all came together during my freshman year of college from a simple observation in a random lunchtime conversation. The subject of fur had come up, and someone remarked that there's little difference between wearing a fur coat and eating meat. The rationale is different—one is for vanity and the other for taste—but they are both unnecessary. There are plenty of coats that can keep you warm and, as I knew from Frances Moore Lappé's groundbreaking book *Diet for a Small Planet*, published six years earlier, a vegetarian diet is healthy.

With this comparison so potently and starkly laid bare, I could no longer avoid the issue. I don't know if I had been in denial or simply never made the connection. But as soon as I heard it articulated, something clicked. The steak on my plate was an animal. It wasn't a piece of meat. It had been a being made of flesh and bone, born into this world, full of emotions, experiencing pleasure and pain. Given a choice, it surely would have chosen life over death.

Even so, the decision was not instantaneous or easy. *I was attached to meat. I didn't want to give it up. I liked it.* It was an important part of my life. But so was being consistent and true to my convictions. If I had compassion for the suffering of animals, if I railed against fur coats, the next step was unavoidable. I became vegetarian.

Evolution of an Advocate

When I became vegetarian and then vegan, people would ask me why. They no longer do; a sure sign veganism has become mainstream. It seems like an easy question, but for me it wasn't. It pushed all sorts of emotional buttons. I confess I didn't handle it well, coming across as self-righteous and argumentative. It didn't help that arguing was a normal part of the culture I was raised in.

It came naturally to me. Holiday dinners were filled with loud arguments crisscrossing the room. It wasn't considered rude or confrontational. It was how my family showed love.

I enjoyed it so much that, after floating through my twenties, I decided to go to law school. Arguing and getting paid for it—what could be better? When I graduated, I had a choice. I could be a highly paid associate at a prestigious law firm a few blocks from the White House or a struggling public defender in Philadelphia representing criminal defendants who couldn't afford an attorney. It wasn't close. Law school had awakened my social consciousness and latent activism, and I knew I would relish the courtroom competition.

*

After three months in Judge Coppolino's courtroom, I knew the signs. A gruff, impatient man, he was happiest when attorneys were arguing angrily with each other. At least once a day he had to vent his own anger at someone, usually an unsuspecting "outside" attorney—not a public defender, like me, or a district attorney—although his wrath could land anywhere. On this particularly slow day, with no victims in sight and his patience reaching its limits, I knew what was coming. Suddenly, out of the blue, he started yelling—at the back wall! After a tirade lasting a full five minutes, his face relaxed, and he leaned back and declared, "I feel better now."

The madness of the situation didn't strike me until a few days later when I made a brief appearance in another courtroom before a different judge with the polar opposite temperament—even-tempered and calm, exactly what you want in a judge. Conditioned by three months of chaos, I was so argumentative that when the judge was ready to rule, he looked at me and declared,

"I was going to rule for your client, but now I'm not so sure." The judge ended up doing the right thing, of course, but the point was made. When I got back to my office, I reflected on not just the past three months but the past 30 years and soon realized my days of arguing were over. I gave notice, left Philadelphia for California, and—following in my parents' footsteps—became a high school teacher in Berkeley.

My answer to the question of why I was vegan also transformed. I became much more attuned to the person I was talking to. Was he sincerely curious or just being polite? Was she receptive or adversarial? Did he want the long answer or the short one? I don't know if it was a strategic decision or the natural result of maturation, but I made a conscious shift from confrontation to engagement.

*

It was a bright, sunny day, and people in the park were treated to a special surprise. Reggie McVeggie, with his frizzy hair, red nose, and oversized shoes, was giving out free vegan burgers. In a few days Vegan Action, the organization for which he was the mascot, would garner international attention when McDonald's threatened to sue for trademark infringement over its "McVegan" T-shirts (a threat McDonald's would eventually withdraw). This group of University of California, Berkeley students had a fresh, upbeat approach, a break from the confrontational posture that characterized much of the animal rights movement. Their message—that veganism is hip—worked, leading all the dorms at Cal to offer vegan options.

My four years as a public defender had argued me out. Leaving teaching to assume leadership of Vegan Action, I embraced its inclusive, positive attitude. Veganism is life-affirming, not life-negating. It made sense for its advocacy to reflect this.

My response to the question "Why vegan?" continued to evolve. Finally, I came to recognize that the best response is the simplest: *"I don't want to hurt animals."*

In the final analysis, this is really what the vegan moral imperative comes down to. On one level the moral question is complicated. That's what this book is about—the psychological processes surrounding the decision to eat or abstain from meat. But at its deepest level, it's quite simple. When you eat meat, animals suffer. Are you okay with that?[*]

"Why Vegetarian?" Revisited

Following that fateful college conversation, my first step on the path to vegetarianism was a clear and open-eyed recognition that *meat is an animal*. While this may seem obvious, it's easy to ignore. The system is designed to obscure the reality. The meat on your plate bears little resemblance to the animal it once was, the language around meat further obfuscates the association, and the entire process is hidden from sight.[†]

Having acknowledged this connection, I could no longer disregard that for me to eat meat, *an animal must be killed*. This thought conjured up the aftermath of my father's death and vivid recollections of the world outside my family room window. I recalled how animals avoid death and cling to life. I understood that

---

[*] In *Eating Animals*, Jonathan Safran Foer recalls how a similar response from a vegetarian babysitter had a profound effect on him.
[†] These and other factors are explored in the second half of the book.

they are involuntary participants in the killing process, suffering and giving up their lives with great reluctance.

Once I accepted the linkage between meat and the killing of an animal, there was an even more difficult reality to confront — my role in it. I didn't kill the animal myself. But somewhere along the causal chain of events was a necessarily violent act — the taking of a life — and *I was a participant in that act*. I was an accomplice, just as culpable as the person who committed it. This is a critical element of the vegan moral imperative. Only by acknowledging our part in the process can we take responsibility for our actions.

The connection between eating meat, animal suffering and death, and the undeniable role we play in it leads to an inescapable fact. *Every time you eat, you are making a moral decision*. It is impossible to be passive. When you buy meat at the supermarket, order meat at a restaurant, or simply eat the meat that your mother, father, spouse, or friend puts on your plate, you are actively harming animals. When you abstain from meat, you are choosing to do no harm. You are either eating ethically, or you are not. There is no morally neutral choice.

Compassion

When faced with suffering, a powerful emotion compels us to action — compassion. Acknowledging the connection between eating meat and harming animals is the first step in rethinking our eating choices. After that, it is compassion that propels us forward, leading us from the fact of animal suffering to the decision to change our behavior. We care. We want to be kind to animals, not hurt them. Compassion is why we give up meat. If their suffering doesn't matter—if we don't care—there is no reason to stop eating them. If it does, there is every reason.

Compassion is the key to the vegan moral imperative, the foundation on which it stands. Compassion is ultimately the cornerstone of any moral philosophy. Without it, we are reduced to completely self-interested beings who consider the interests of others only insofar as they further our own. A morality without compassion is no morality at all, and a life without morality is no life at all. I truly believe that when we look at the situation clear-eyed and with open, generous hearts, we give up eating meat quite naturally.

Why Vegan?

As I navigated through my twenties, experimenting with different career paths—professional blackjack player (aka card counter) in Las Vegas, computer programmer and realtor in Atlanta—vegetarianism remained largely in the background of my life. That changed suddenly my first year of law school when PETA (People for the Ethical Treatment of Animals) put on an exhibit in the school's lobby. I was shocked. I knew nothing about "factory farms" or the cruel and inhumane conditions under which animals are raised. I was unaware of the inextricable link between the meat and dairy industries.

The decision to go vegan was harder than the one to become vegetarian. I knew my girlfriend would not approve, so it would add stress to a relationship already strained by distance and the pressures of law school and, for her, medical school. More than that, I really, really did not want to give up cheese. A life without pizza, or ice cream for that matter, seemed unimaginable. But as before, faced with a moral dilemma, the outcome was inevitable. I became vegan.

When you think of a farm, you might envision an idyllic setting of pastures and lakes where animals live out their lives peacefully and die a quick, painless death. The reality is strikingly different. Of the estimated 70 billion farmed animals killed worldwide every year for food, two-thirds are reared on factory farms,[1] where conditions are horrific.

Factory farms are mass-production machines whose sole concern is profit. The cows, pigs, chickens, sheep, and other animals lead short, miserable lives. In the egg industry, hens spend their entire lives in small cages with so little room to move that their toes sometimes grow around the wiring. Female chicks have their beaks cut off so they don't peck each other to death in these cramped quarters. Male chicks are killed at birth—either electrocuted, ground up alive, suffocated, or gassed.

Dairy cows have their tails docked and are kept continuously impregnated. Genetically manipulated to produce ten to twelve times the amount of milk needed to nourish their offspring, they frequently suffer from mastitis, a painful swelling of the udders. Cows can live up to twenty years, but on factory farms dairy cows become spent by the age of four and, no longer useful, are killed for meat.

Like humans, cows form a strong bond with their calves, but on factory farms mother and baby are forcibly separated, usually within the first twenty-four hours. They can be heard crying as they frantically look for each other. Calves slated for veal are tied to a post or confined to a crate for the entirety of their short lives and fed an anemic diet to ensure their meat is pale and tender. Calves raised for meat are frequently dehorned, castrated, and branded, in many cases without painkillers. At about a year old they are sent to a feedlot, fattened on an unnatural corn-rich diet, and slaughtered, with one guideline suggesting an even earlier death—"between three and 16 weeks of age" to produce the "highest quality beef."[2]

I remember a poignant moment in India, where cows often roam the streets freely. I was walking through an outdoor marketplace in Agra after touring the Taj Mahal, when I heard a distant bleat, followed by a moo. The bleating and mooing continued, getting closer and closer to each other. I arrived just in time to witness the happy reunion of mother and calf, who had been separated by the swarm of people, as she joyously licked his face. This tender scene stands in stark contrast to the desolate life of cows and their offspring on factory farms.

Pigs are extremely intelligent and sensitive.[3] Yet within weeks of their birth they are castrated and have their tails cut off, all without anesthetic. The confinement of sows in small crates for their entire lives is both physical and psychological torture for these highly social animals.

Most people don't know that in the United States two-thirds of the fish we eat comes from factory farms—called aquaculture—where conditions are likewise atrocious. The fish can't move and live in water contaminated by excrement, antibiotics, and pesticides, which also pollute surrounding water. These fish farms are highly inefficient, taking five pounds of codfish or other fishes (used as feed) to make one pound of the pricier farmed fish.

You may think the terms "free-range" and "organic" mean the animals are raised in humane conditions. These are very misleading. Free-range chickens, while not in cages, can still be crammed into windowless warehouses. They are debeaked and killed at a young age, like their caged counterparts, and it is not required to render them unconscious for the slaughtering process. Cows in organic farms face the same cycle of impregnation and premature slaughter as factory farmed cows, and their babies also are taken away at birth, the males sold for beef or veal. Patti Breitman, author of three vegan books and cofounder of Dharma Voices for Animals, talks about "humane" farming:

> [Factory farming] is the polar opposite of compassion for all living beings....
>
> There's a new movement afoot called humane farming, and a lot of people think that as long as I'm eating animals that come from humane farms, that's okay. You may have heard the terms cage-free, free-range, pasture-fed, humane. All of those terms mean absolutely nothing.... Even on a "humane" farm, there's really no such thing as humane farming.[4]

Will Tuttle, author of *The World Peace Diet*, describes these farms:

> [I]n some ways free-range and organic farms are more harmful. Organic farms can't use antibiotics so they can't treat medical conditions such as mastitis—inflammation of the udder—instead using mechanical instruments to re-mouth the teats. Overall there is more violence and abuse in organic and free-range farms.[5]

This overview touches briefly on the horrific conditions on modern-day factory farms. If you're interested in learning more about these inhumane operations, there are documentaries like *Food, Inc.* and books like *Animal Factories*, which offer detailed accounts of the cruelties to which the animals are routinely subjected.

The reason for going vegan, on top of going vegetarian, was succinctly stated by renowned animal law attorney Gary Francione. "There is probably more suffering in a glass of milk than in a pound of steak." Knowing this, the simple answer to "Why vegan?" is the same as to "Why vegetarian?": *"I don't want to hurt animals."*

Compassion Toward Humans

When I first became vegan, I often defaulted to an attitude of certitude, moral superiority, and insistence. This is common among "true believers," as I've witnessed firsthand in activism, religion, and politics, all of which tend to elicit passion. My posture transformed over time, fueled by both strategic considerations and personal growth.

During my twenties, as I struggled to find the right balance between my activist tendencies and my argumentative nature, I came across Dale Carnegie's *How to Win Friends and Influence People*. I don't generally read this type of book, but its impact was profound, helping me recognize how many of the ways I interacted with people were counterproductive. One of its main points, obvious to me now, is that people don't want to be told what to do. If your goal is to convince others, show them the way. Don't try to pull them there by the nose. After reading it, I eliminated the phrase "you should" from my vocabulary.

My understanding of self-righteousness took longer to evolve. Part of it was the recognition that none of us—me included—is morally pure. There's always room to grow. We can always do better. Until we're saints, we have no basis to judge others. Once we become saints, we have no desire to judge others.

By the same token, no one has a monopoly on wisdom. Our certitude must be countered by the possibility, in every decision made and opinion held, that we may be *wrong*. As strongly as I believe in the correctness of my views, others see things differently with equal fervor. How do I know I'm right? We're all limited by our own perspectives. Maybe the other person is the one who sees things clearly. When we accept our fallibility, conviction is tempered by humility.

Ori, a vegan we'll meet in chapter eight, weighs in on this:

> *I don't think assigning blame is useful.... I think that sitting there and judging others for not doing this, not doing this, not doing this, isn't particularly useful. It's actually kind of counterproductive.... I don't know if there is a strict morality whatsoever, and I think to pretend to know it is very dangerous.*

Every life is an evolution. No one is born on the finish line. When talking about veganism, or anything for that matter, I realized you have to meet people where they are, not where you want them to be. In confronting limitations—whether our own or others'—growth is nurtured by celebrating the progress we make rather than condemning the shortcomings we have yet to overcome. Change happens only when we're ready.

The most important lesson I've learned is also the most difficult to practice. Compassion extends to all beings—human and nonhuman alike—*even to people doing harm.* It's not easy putting this into action when you witness cruelty, but it may help to recognize that when people do harm, it is because they themselves are in pain. People at total inner peace—if any exist—are incapable of intentionally harming others. The slaughterhouse worker, inflicting so much suffering, is suffering himself—even if he isn't aware of it. This is framed by some religious traditions as "hate the act but love the actor." Both of these feelings can be held simultaneously—and they must, if we are to be true to our compassionate nature.

What's in a Name?

The intelligent, contemplative man and his group of his followers gazed at the geometric figure before them, as they had done so often. There was something special about the relationship between the sides of this unique shape, but they couldn't quite put their finger on it. Finally, imagining the sides as squares and applying known laws of congruent triangles, they made their discovery: when you take the square of one leg of the right triangle and add the square of the other, you end up with the square of the hypotenuse. As Archimedes might have exclaimed, "Eureka!"

The moral question of eating animals is not new. In the West it dates back at least 2,500 years to a man whose name is familiar to anyone who has ever taken high school geometry. Discoverer of the eponymous Pythagorean theorem, $a^2 + b^2 = c^2$, Pythagoras was more than a brilliant mathematician. He was the founder of a society, called the Pythagoreans, that strongly influenced ancient

Greek society and profoundly shaped the course of Western civilization. Pythagoreans were also excellent athletes and welcomed women into their ranks, a progressive practice that boldly challenged the sexist status quo of their time.

Pythagoras believed in metempsychosis, or transmigration of souls, often referred to as reincarnation. Since an animal could be the reincarnation of a human, Pythagoreans abstained from meat so that they wouldn't harm someone they had once known. This stood in contrast to the teachings of Aristotle, whose hierarchical approach to ethics held that lower beings, as he defined them, exist for the benefit of higher beings. According to Aristotle, animals are here to serve man. While Aristotle won the day—and the next 2,500 years—Pythagoras's influence remained. In fact, until the mid-nineteenth century the word "vegetarian" did not exist in English. Vegetarians were called Pythagoreans.

The word "vegan" was coined in 1944 by Donald Watson, founder of the Vegan Society in the United Kingdom, taking the first and last letters of the word "vegetarian." The unprecedented level of suffering inflicted by the meat and dairy industry necessitated a new way of eating—along with a new word to describe it. While it had once arguably been enough merely to abstain from meat, the cruelty of modern animal agriculture made veganism, not just vegetarianism, a moral imperative.

The moral case for vegetarianism has recurred throughout history. Among its adherents have been Plato, Leonardo da Vinci, Leo Tolstoy, Annie Besant, Mahatma Gandhi, Louisa May Alcott, George Bernard Shaw, Mary Shelley, Percy Shelley, Dr. John Harvey Kellogg, Albert Einstein and Cesar Chavez. Alcott and Chavez were vegan, as was Gandhi at one point in his life, writing in his autobiography, "I had long realized that milk was not necessary for supporting the body, but it was not easy to give up.... I happened to come across some literature from Calcutta, describing the tortures to which cows and buffaloes were subjected by their keepers." When his friend suggested they give it up, they "pledged ourselves to abjure milk then and there."[6] Martin Luther King, Jr., strongly influenced by Gandhi, was not a vegetarian, but his wife, Coretta Scott King, and son Dexter Scott King became vegan, suggesting he too might have moved in that direction had his life not been tragically cut short. Today, any number of thinkers, entertainers, athletes, politicians, and others are self-described vegetarians and vegans.[*]

The Philosophy

Just as *Silent Spring* is often cited as having launched the environmental movement, the modern animal rights/welfare movement is commonly traced back to Peter Singer's 1975 classic *Animal Liberation*. Singer employs a utilitarian approach to ethics, where the morally superior choice is that which maximizes overall pleasure and minimizes overall pain.

Singer's philosophy rests on the notion of equal consideration of interests, which stem from the capacity to suffer or to experience pleasure. If a being suffers, that suffering must be taken into account and treated equally, regardless of species. It is the suffering that counts, not who is suffering. Since the animals we eat suffer and experience pleasure, they have interests and must be included in our moral construct. Singer writes, "The good of any

---

[*] For an excellent treatise on the history of vegetarianism since 1600, I recommend Tristram Stuart's *The Bloodless Revolution*.

one individual is of no more importance, from the point of view (if I may say so) of the Universe, than the good of any other." Conversely, in the absence of the capacity for suffering or pleasure, it makes no sense to talk of interests. "The capacity for suffering and enjoyment is *a prerequisite for having interests at all.*"[7] For Singer, sentience is the boundary of our moral concern. I strongly recommend this groundbreaking book, which also includes discussion of factory farms, vivisection, and speciesism, a mindset we'll explore in chapter four that Singer compares to sexism and racism.

Another landmark modern treatment of this subject is Tom Regan's *The Case for Animal Rights*. Regan rejects utilitarianism, relying instead on a rights view of morality, in which every individual has inherent value that must be respected. Moral relevancy applies to all beings who are "subjects of a life," which means having beliefs and desires, perception, memory, a sense of the future, an emotional life with feelings of pleasure and pain, and several other attributes.[8] Written as a philosophical dissertation, the book does not lend itself to casual perusal. It's geared toward those interested in a more rigorous approach to moral philosophy.

The book *The Feminist Care Tradition in Animal Ethics* advances feminist ethic-of-care theory, a concept first put forth in 1982 by Carol Gilligan. "The feminist ethic of care regards animals as individuals who do have feelings, who can communicate those feelings, and to whom therefore humans have moral obligations."[9] Feminist care theorists explicitly distinguish it from the animal rights and utilitarian theories of Regan and Singer, rejecting many of their premises. Characterizing these "men's 'conceptions of morality'" as relying on fairness, rights, and rules and dispensing with sympathy, empathy, and compassion, feminist care theory posits a "women's 'conception of morality'" based on caring, responsibility, and relationships. In place of abstraction and generality, feminist care theory considers the particulars of a case, recognizes the heterogeneity of life, and is attuned to the political and economic systems responsible for animal suffering. Reflecting feminism more widely, it rejects "hierarchical dominative dualisms" that establish the dominant over the subordinate.

"Zoopolis," a term coined in 1998 by Jennifer Wolch, is a more recent model that employs a political framework. In *Zoopolis: A Political Theory of Animal Rights*, authors Sue Donaldson and Will Kymlicka propose an animal rights theory that combines traditional notions of inviolable rights based on sentience with obligations stemming from our relationship to animals. This construct classifies animals into three distinct groups—animals in the wild having separate sovereign communities, liminal opportunistic animals (such as raccoons) who move into areas inhabited by humans, and domesticated animals. It then applies principles of citizenship to these groups to determine our duties toward them.[10]

Animals in Religion

"And God said, Behold, I have given you every herb bearing seed, which is upon the face of all the earth, and every tree, in which is the fruit of a tree yielding fruit; to you it shall be for meat." (Genesis 1:29)

It is generally accepted that the Judeo-Christian tradition does not mandate vegetarianism, but advocates can find scriptural support in the Bible. The above quote reveals that in the beginning humans were vegetarians. Permission to eat meat is not granted until Genesis 9, when humans have become so depraved that God unleashes the great flood, killing everyone except Noah and his family. God decides to never cause such a flood again, but he lowers his moral standards for humans, allowing them to eat meat.

The Peaceable Kingdom of Isaiah 11:6–9, where "the wolf shall live with the lamb," is a further source of inspiration for some Christian vegetarians. According to the Talmud, Judaism has a commandment called *Tza'ar ba'alei Chayim* ("the suffering of animals") that requires people not only to prevent unnecessary animal suffering but to proactively relieve it when they can. Kosher laws, meant to minimize suffering, reflect the Bible's compassion toward animals. Matthew Scully's *Dominion* is an excellent source for a biblical perspective on veganism.[11]

*

One day the Vedic sage Narma Muni is walking through the forest when he sees a wounded deer, injured by an arrow. Soon thereafter he comes upon a bird struck by an arrow, still alive. As he walks, he sees more and more animals pierced by arrows, slowly dying. He becomes upset and wonders: Who is doing this? When he meets the hunter Magira, Narma Muni begs him to stop the cruelty. Magira replies that his family has always hunted to make its living. But why is he injuring and not killing the animals? That's how he was taught. The sage then explains that humans don't have to create such suffering—they don't have to kill at all. The hunter is skeptical, not believing such a society exists.

Finally, Magira is convinced and agrees to stop hunting on one condition—that Narma Muni take on the responsibility of caring for and feeding Magira and his family. Narma Muni has Magira renounce the world, telling him people will come to him offering food that is not from the killing of animals. Magira begins meditating, practicing compassion, and following Narma Muni's advice. The locals come and make offerings so that Magira and his wife can be vegetarians. They end up living happy, cruelty-free lives.

Eastern philosophy has always resonated with me, perhaps because of its treatment of animals. Hinduism, the source of the above story, is a vegetarian religion, guided by the principle of *ahimsa*, or nonviolence. Cows are sacred in India, where you can see them asleep in the middle of the road, cars and buses desperately trying to avoid hitting them, lest the drivers accrue bad karma. Inexplicably, this same compassion does not extend to the countless homeless dogs and cats who roam the streets and are treated very poorly. There's a sad but telling saying: "If you're a cow, you want to be born in India and not the West. If you're a dog, you want to be born in the West and not India."

Jainism, another Eastern religion based on *ahimsa* and compassion, is the strictest with regard to not killing. The Jain leader Mahavira, a contemporary of the Buddha, believed that the weightiest types of karma come from killing, including killing animals. The only way to attain freedom from *samsara*—the cycle of birth and rebirth—is to live an existence completely devoid of harming. Strict Jains live off fruits, vegetables, and other "one-sensed" life forms and adhere to a number of fastidious practices that foster nonkilling, such as not eating in the dark, checking clothes for insects, and carefully avoiding accidentally stepping on them.

When I first started meditating and studying Buddhism twenty-two years ago, I was elated when I came upon the First Precept: abstain from killing. One of five guiding moral principles for laypeople, it is universally understood to include animals. Thomas Tryon, a British vegetarian of the 1600s, had a similar experience. "When Tryon heard the rumours of Indians living with the animals he was transfixed with joy; vegetarianism was no longer relegated to the backwaters of English religious dissidence—it was the creed followed by entire nations of herb-eaters like himself."[12]

My joy turned to chagrin when I subsequently learned that many, if not most, Buddhists eat meat and that there is even disagreement over whether the Buddha was a vegetarian. The two main Buddhist lineages, Mahayana and Theravada, have very different takes on this. Mahayana Buddhism, which includes Tibetan and Zen, is certain that the Buddha was vegetarian and that he prescribed a vegetarian diet. In the sutras, or discourses, given over his forty-five-year ministry, the Buddha repeatedly prohibits eating meat. In one sutra he says, "Animal flesh eating is forbidden by Me everywhere and for all time for those who abide in compassion."[13] No one disagrees that meat is forbidden in Mahayana Buddhism, even nonvegetarians like the Dalai Lama.

Theravada Buddhism is less clear. Its adherents who eat meat justify the practice by relying on a principle referred to as the three purities, which allows monks to eat meat if it was neither seen, heard, nor suspected that the animal was killed for the monk.* In some discourses the Buddha purportedly eats meat himself. If the Buddha did in fact enunciate this doctrine, the rationale is not clear. It appears to balance the need for maintaining harmonious relations with the laity, on whom monks depended (and still depend) for food, with the principle of not killing animals. Given the entirety of the Theravada teachings and their emphasis on compassion toward all beings, including animals, I have doubts about

---

* This instruction was given to monks. Its applicability to laypeople is questionable.

the authenticity of the three purities doctrine. Several years ago, I cofounded the nonprofit organization Dharma Voices for Animals, dedicated to promoting veganism within the meditation and broader Buddhist communities, and I refer you to its website for an extended discussion of this subject.[14] I also recommend the film *Animals and the Buddha*, which you can watch on YouTube.[15]

Buddhism provides another rationale for vegetarianism that may seem familiar from our discussion of Pythagoras. In one discourse the Buddha explains that over the course of our rebirths, spanning back through beginningless time, we have been related to every being: "A being who has not been your mother [father, brother, sister, son, daughter] at one time in the past is not easy to find."[16] The cow you are about to eat was, at some point, a family member, and we don't eat family members.

It's conjectured that Pythagoras, a frequent traveler, reached India and was influenced by Eastern religion. If so, a subtle but critical point suggests it was Hinduism rather than Buddhism. The Hindu notion of reincarnation, where the soul is born into a new body, differs from the Buddhist notion of not-self, which posits rebirth but denies the existence of a soul. Pythagoras's articulation of metempsychosis reflects a Hindu perspective.

*

I became a vegan for moral reasons, and the vegan moral imperative remains decisive. There is no escaping the fact that when we eat meat and animal products, we are complicit in the suffering and killing of beings who are intelligent and highly sensitive and who value their lives as much as we value ours. Eating necessarily involves a moral decision, and compassion leads us to choose veganism.

Chapter 2:

The Environmental Imperative

When she was fifteen, Emily read Animal Liberation *for a paper she was writing on animal experimentation. She became vegetarian the next day. At the University of Vermont she started the first animal rights group and learned more about the impact of animal agriculture. This led to a career in environmental protection, including working as the recycling coordinator for the city of Burlington, earning a graduate degree at the Harvard Kennedy School, working for the World Bank and State Department, working as finance director of a congressional campaign, and serving as the Massachusetts director for the Sierra Club. She is currently the executive director of the Charles River Watershed Association as well as a councilperson in Newton, Massachusetts.*

Emily talks about the environmental impact of animal agriculture:

> *Meat harms the environment in so many ways. It takes a lot more land to be cleared for animal agriculture. Basically it's just more inefficient to feed plants to animals and then to us rather than to eat the plant material ourselves. You look at the deforestation of the Amazon. All of that is related to clearing land for beef production. The immense amount of air pollution and water pollution from these manure lagoons is just horrible for the environment. The energy and water that goes into the animal agriculture industry is significant.... In fact, in the whole planet there's not enough arable land to*

> *support the current human population eating the way Americans do.*

Emily went vegan but started eating a little dairy again when she was pregnant. While she has almost entirely given it up, using substitutes like soy ice cream and vegan cheese, her one indulgence is cow's milk in her latte, the one place where coconut, soy, and oat milk just don't work for her. Her three sons are vegetarians.

*

If I weren't vegan for moral reasons, I'd be vegan for environmental ones. Years ago I heard a radio interview with a man who had reduced his nonbiodegradable waste to something like one compact cubic foot a year. At the time I dismissed it as eccentricity, but I remembered it. Over the years, as my environmental awareness has grown, I've come to fully appreciate the wisdom of his undertaking. We sometimes treat the earth as if its resources are unlimited and its resiliency unbounded. They're not.

I happen to be a nature lover. I grew up in it. I live in it. I've backpacked some of the most beautiful places in the United States—Zion, the Grand Canyon, Big Bend, the Adirondacks, the Blue Ridge Mountains, Yosemite, Emigrant Wilderness. Living in the heart of Redwood Country in Northern California, I've experienced daily the splendor of these majestic trees. But you don't have to love the environment to appreciate its importance, just as you don't have to love animals to have compassion and respect for them. The earth sustains us. It is the ultimate source of our food, whether vegan or animal-based.

Part of my environmental awareness is the recognition that whenever I use resources, it impacts the environment. I visited my friend Mindy, who works for an environmental organization, after she bought a house. Giving me the tour, she pointed to her new sofa resignedly and apologetically. All the furniture in her house was used, with this one exception that her mother insisted on buying her. In some areas, society can be credited with taking action. Fueled by concerns about finite resources and pollution, recycling is now standard. For the same reasons, many people have cut back on buying plastic, driving, flying, using water, and other activities.

In many ways, the environmental consequences of eating meat are the driving force behind the current vegan trend. Animal agriculture is environmentally devastating, contributing to global warming, deforestation, pollution, unsafe water, and hunger, among other ills. Yet despite the urgency of these problems, our response is slow and inadequate, in part because of limits to how much we can or are willing to change our behavior. Few of us have the time or dedication to go as far as that man on the radio. But when given the opportunity to minimize our imprint and protect the environment, we can seize it. Going vegan is one change each of us can make in an instant with profound positive implications for the earth.

In exploring this subject, I try to minimize statistics, since I know they can be off-putting, but sometimes they're the only way to tell the story. If you happen to like numbers, the website of the documentary *Cowspiracy* is a statistician's dream, each fact diligently supported.[17]

Global Warming

As part of the show's long-standing commitment to sustainable practices, the 26th Annual Screen Actors Guild Awards will feature a plant-based menu at its ceremony on Sunday, January 19th. The SAG Awards has been the recipient of the Environmental Media Association (EMA) Green Seal for 11 years running in addition to having been awarded the EMA Gold Seal and the Green Production honor. The SAG Awards has also partnered for multiple years with non-profit environmental organizations such as American Forests. For the 25th Anniversary of the SAG Awards, American Forests planted 25,000 trees across the U.S. in a collaborative effort to improve the quality of air, water and wildlife habitat.[18]

The above announcement for the 2020 SAG Awards, following the lead set by the Golden Globes, is one of many signs that awareness of the environmental harm caused by a meat-based diet—catalyzed by apprehension about global warming and sustainability—has entered mainstream consciousness. The fashion industry is following suit, as reported by CNN:

Vegan sneakers set to be next sustainable plant-based craze in 2020

Experts say next year's game-changing trend in sustainable consumer goods may be plant-based — or "vegan" — athletic shoes.

Last week, Reebok, owned by Adidas (ADDDF) since 2005, unveiled the design for its first plant-based running shoe, the Floatride GROW, which is expected to hit store shelves in the fall of 2020....

In August, Nike, Adidas and Puma joined 30 other apparel companies as signatories on the G7 Fashion Pact, which French Prime Minister Emmanuel Macron unveiled at the annual G7 Summit. Nike has also committed to reducing its carbon footprint by 30% by 2030 through its partnership with the UN Framework Convention on Climate Change.[19]

---

*

I first became aware of global warming in 2006 from the book *An Inconvenient Truth* by former vice president and current vegan Al Gore. In researching this topic, I was astonished to learn that the first alarm bells were rung over a century ago, in 1896, when scientist Svante Arrhenius theorized about the greenhouse effect and global warming. In the 1930s steam engineer Guy Stewart Callendar postulated that increased carbon dioxide in the atmosphere could lead to rising temperatures. In the 1970s actually rising global temperatures led to predictions about global warming, which went unheeded.

Another landmark came on June 23, 1988, when the congressional testimony of Dr. James Hansen, director of the NASA Goddard Institute for Space Studies, received national attention. Dr. Hansen summarized his three main conclusions:

> Number one, the earth is warmer in 1988 than at any time in the history of instrumental measurements. Number two, the global warming is now large enough that we can ascribe with a high degree of confidence a cause and effect relationship to the greenhouse effect. And number three, our computer climate simulations indicate that the greenhouse effect is already large enough to begin to effect the probability of extreme events such as summer heat waves.[20]

That same year the United Nations created the Intergovernmental Panel on Climate Change (IPCC), whose role was "to assess on a comprehensive, objective, open and transparent basis the scientific, technical and socio-economic information relevant to understanding the scientific basis of risk of human-induced climate change, its potential impacts and options for adaptation and mitigation."[21] The IPCC and Gore shared the 2007 Nobel Peace Prize for their work on climate change.

The 2014 IPCC assessment report reached several ominous conclusions:

> Human influence on the climate system is clear, and recent anthropogenic emissions of greenhouse gases are the highest in history. Recent climate

changes have had widespread impacts on human and natural systems.

Warming of the climate system is unequivocal, and since the 1950s, many of the observed changes are unprecedented over decades to millennia. The atmosphere and ocean have warmed, the amounts of snow and ice have diminished, and sea level has risen.

Continued emission of greenhouse gases will cause further warming and long-lasting changes in all components of the climate system, increasing the likelihood of severe, pervasive and irreversible impacts for people and ecosystems. Limiting climate change would require substantial and sustained reductions in greenhouse gas emissions which, together with adaptation, can limit climate change risks.[22]

Extreme weather events are increasing in intensity and frequency seemingly before our eyes, with formerly once-in-a-lifetime occurrences now commonplace. The congressionally mandated U.S. Global Change Research Program finds, "Human-induced climate change has already increased the number and strength of some of these extreme events. Over the last 50 years, much of the United States has seen an increase in prolonged periods of excessively high temperatures, more heavy downpours, and in some regions, more severe droughts."[23] According to the U.S. government's National Centers for Environmental Information, 2020 was the second-warmest year on record, and "The seven warmest years ... have all occurred since 2014, while the 10 warmest years have occurred since 2005."[24]

The U.S. military fully understands the threat, writing in a 2015 report:

> [The Department of Defense] recognizes the reality of climate change and the significant risk it poses to U.S. interests globally. The National Security Strategy, issued in February 2015, is clear that climate change is an urgent and growing threat to our national security, contributing to increased natural disasters, refugee flows, and conflicts over basic resources such as food and water.[25]

The verdict is in. Global warming is an existential threat, not just to humans but to virtually every species on earth. Among the stated goals of the 2015 Paris Agreement, adopted at the United Nations Climate Change Conference and now ratified by 189 countries, was "holding the increase in the global average temperature to well below 2°C above pre-industrial levels and pursuing efforts to limit the temperature increase to 1.5°C above pre-industrial levels, recognizing that this would significantly reduce the risks and impacts of climate change."[26]

Living in Northern California, global warming is not a theoretical issue for me. As I wrote this book, record-breaking forest fires raged to my north, east, and south. During one stretch the air was unhealthy for two straight weeks, the smoke blocking the sun for days on end and ash falling from the sky. Not long ago, at the height of the drought, water rationing was in effect. Absent radical action, we are not likely to reach the goal of the Paris Agreement, and the long-term consequences will be dire.

*

The main cause of global warming is the emission of greenhouse gases into the atmosphere. These gases—primarily carbon dioxide, methane, and nitrous oxide—trap heat, which warms the planet. Animal agriculture produces greenhouse gases in four main ways:

- Enteric fermentation, the production of methane by animals' digestive systems, accounts for more than a third of global methane emissions.

- Feed production, including deforestation to clear land for grazing and feed crops, generates almost half of the gases associated with animal agriculture.

- Manure management releases an enormous amount of methane and nitrous oxide.

- The overall production process requires energy consumption at all stages, from the use of machinery for feed crops to the transportation of animals to market.[27]

One statistic encapsulates the vegan environmental imperative: animal agriculture accounts for between 14.5 and 18 percent of all greenhouse gas emissions in the world—more than the transportation sector.[28] Looked at another way, **eating meat* contributes more to global warming than driving your car.**

---

* For the remainder of the book, unless the context indicates otherwise, the word "meat" is intended to include meat, dairy, eggs, and other animal products.

Most people recognize the collective nature of the problem. Unlike the morality of eating meat, where our individual role may seem inconsequential, with the environment we intuitively understand that everyone makes a difference. It's why we recycle, reuse bags, drive less, buy electric cars, and take other actions to reduce our environmental footprints. A study in the United Kingdom found that a meat-based diet produces 2.5 times as many greenhouse gas emissions as a vegan one.[29] Giving up meat is the most important contribution we can make to reducing global warming.

Land/Hunger

"Why, land is the only thing in the world worth workin' for, worth fightin' for, worth dyin' for, because it's the only thing that lasts."
    Gerald O'Hara, *Gone With the Wind*

Land was a focal point of human conflict long before we started raising animals for food. Animal agriculture has exacerbated the problem. As Tristram Stuart discusses, 2,400 years ago Plato—a vegetarian—observed that "the demand for meat increased land hunger and thus led to disputes with neighbouring people."[30] Concerns were raised in the fifteenth and sixteenth centuries that using arable land for sheep pastures to supply the wool industry was "depopulating the countryside." In the late 1700s, when Europe faced food shortages due to surging population growth, people like the Reverend William Paley sounded the alarm, pointing out the massive inefficiency of raising animals for meat: "[A] piece of ground capable of supplying animal food sufficient for the subsistence of ten persons would sustain, at least, double that number with grain, roots, and milk."

Until that time, there had been no meat industry per se in Europe. Instead, "meat was principally a by-product of agricultural systems in which animals were reared on otherwise unusable land and fed waste products."[31] Male calves and mothers no longer producing milk were killed so they wouldn't consume resources. Everything changed with the birth of the meat industry. Grain was now grown specifically for animals, fundamentally transforming the landscape. In the United States, "animal husbandry was developed through experience at first, but in the latter half of the 19th century, leaders of government recognized the need to further develop its agriculture, for only an efficient agriculture could free labor to develop a great nation."[32]

Again, one statistic about modern animal agriculture is telling: "In all, livestock production accounts for 70 percent of all agricultural land and 30 percent of the land surface of the planet."[33] This is not worth working, fighting, or dying for.

*

When I was a kid, world hunger was making headlines. To prompt me to finish what was on my plate, my mother would tell me there were people starving in Africa. I didn't quite get it, since I *always* ate *everything*. I also didn't understand how my eating had anything to do with people in Africa.

World hunger is a complex issue, not simply a question of available food. The world produces enough food to feed everyone. But because of meat's inefficiency—it requires eighteen times the land area used to grow the plants in a vegan diet[34]—and high demand, resources that would otherwise go to stop hunger are diverted to meat production. Half of all grain produced world-wide is consumed by farmed animals.*

The dominance of animal agriculture creates scarcity, causing the price of land and water to increase. Poor people who might otherwise have access to these resources can't afford them. Around 1800 Erasmus Darwin argued, "Since pasturage actually produced less food and employed fewer people, this quest for profit was responsible for emptying whole villages and starving the poor into slavery."[35] Today, over 80 percent of starving children live in countries where food goes to animals who are eaten by people in wealthier countries like the United States. "One fourth of all grain produced by third-world countries is now given to livestock, in their own countries and elsewhere. Therefore, on a local basis, animal-based agriculture simply perpetuates hunger, poverty ... illiteracy ... and poor human health."[36]

My mother was right after all.

Deforestation

In 2019 the world watched in horror as large swaths of the Amazon rainforest, the most biodiverse area on the planet, burned before our very eyes. The fires were not naturally occurring or a one-off event. The Amazon is regularly set ablaze to make way for pastureland for cows and crops for the meat industry. In 2000 a project was launched to assess the impacts of animal agriculture on the global environment. Coordinated by the Food

---

* I prefer "farmed animals" to the term "livestock," which implies animals are nothing more than commodities. It is also preferable to "farm animals," which suggests a type of animal whose nature is to be farmed and eaten.

and Agricultural Organization of the United Nations and supported by a consortium of international organizations, in 2006 the
Livestock, Environment and Development (LEAD) Initiative concluded, "Expansion of livestock production is a key factor in deforestation, especially in Latin America where the greatest
amount of deforestation is occurring—70 percent of previous forested land in the Amazon is occupied by pastures, and feedcrops
cover a large part of the remainder."[37]

The Union of Concerned Scientists finds that "of the four
major deforestation drivers, beef has by far the largest impact"
and explains deforestation's impact on climate change: "Forests—
especially tropical forests—store enormous amounts of carbon.
When forests are destroyed, that carbon is released to the atmosphere, accelerating global warming."[38]

The resultant loss of wildlife habitat portends another huge
crisis—mass extinction. According to the Intergovernmental
Science-Policy Platform on Biodiversity and Ecosystem Services:

> **Human actions threaten more species with global
> extinction now than ever before.** An average of
> around 25 per cent of species in assessed animal
> and plant groups are threatened, suggesting that
> around 1 million species already face extinction,
> many within decades, unless action is taken to re-
> duce the intensity of drivers of biodiversity loss.
> Without such action, there will be a further accel-
> eration in the global rate of species extinction,
> which is already at least tens to hundreds of times
> higher than it has averaged over the past 10 million
> years.[39]

Wildlife is also targeted directly. To appease ranchers and farmers, the U.S. Department of Agriculture kills millions of animals every year—coyotes, bears, bobcats, mountain lions, beavers, otters, buffaloes, horses, geese, swans, skunks, prairie dogs, squirrels, wrens, blackbirds, starlings, and eagles—by poisoning, shooting, or trapping them. Not long ago, activists in my community in rural California tried to stop the killing, proposing a nonlethal alternative. After a years-long campaign and intense public hearing, it was voted down 3–2 by the county's board of supervisors, testament to the power of animal agriculture interests.

Water

Some years ago, I spent five and a half months meditating at a monastery in Sri Lanka. It was an idyllic setting, the *kutis* (*kuti* means hut or dwelling—this monastery was known for its cave *kutis* built into the rocks) spread throughout a rainforest shared with bands of monkeys and other indigenous wildlife. My *kuti* had a spigot outside for washing, but for drinking water I would fill my two liter bottles every morning at the dining hall, a ten-minute walk away.

Maybe because of this, every so often when I turn on my kitchen faucet, I appreciate how lucky I am. I know that for much of the world water is a scarce resource. According to the United Nations, 30 percent of the world's population does not have access to safe drinking water, and for four billion people, water is severely scarce at least one month out of every year.[40]

The situation will only get worse, with worldwide water use expected to rise 20 to 30 percent by 2050. The meat industry's inefficient use of water is a major contributor to the problem. Again, the statistics are shocking: *it takes 2,500 gallons of water to produce one pound of beef and 420 gallons to produce one pound of grain-fed broiler chicken; per pound, beef uses more than 20 times as much water as soybeans, 25 times as much as rice, and 65 times as much as corn.*[41]

Excessive use of a scarce resource is only one aspect of the problem. Once used, the water does not simply evaporate or get absorbed by the animals. Most of it returns to the environment in the form of excrement or wastewater. The U.S. General Accounting Office explains that animal waste runoff contains pollutants such as nitrogen and phosphorous, organic matter, sediments, pathogens (including bacteria and viruses), heavy metals, hormones, antibiotics, and ammonia. Rainwater, snowmelt, and irrigation water transport these pollutants to rivers, lakes, coastal waters, and groundwater, contaminating drinking water and killing fish.[42]

Slaughterhouses, meat-processing plants, dairies, and tanneries are also significant sources of local water pollution due to runoff from processing areas and direct discharge of wastewater into freshwater. We also saw this with fish factory farms, where excrement and chemicals leak into nearby water.

The LEAD Initiative, devoting a chapter to this subject, concludes, "Overall, summing up the impacts of all the different segments of the production chain, the livestock sector has an enormous impact on water use, water quality, hydrology and aquatic ecosystems."[43]

Pollution

Driving down Interstate 5 in California, your eyes don't have to be open to know you've reached Coalinga. The stench from the stockyards lining the highway is unmistakable. Two of the main culprits are ammonia and hydrogen sulfide, but these factory farms emit over one hundred gases, including carbon monoxide, chlorofluorocarbons, ammonia, nitrogen oxides, and sulfur dioxide. When these last two come in contact with atmospheric moisture and oxidants, they convert to sulfuric and nitric acids, which are noxious to human and animal respiratory systems. They return to earth as acid rain and snow and dry deposited gases and particles, damaging crops and forests and making lakes and streams unsuitable for plant and animal life.[44]

A dead zone is a hypoxic pocket in a body of water—an area where the oxygen level is so low it can kill fish and other marine life. These zones are lethal and widespread, due in large part to the meat and dairy industry. The Pew Commission on Industrial Farm Animal Production finds, "Agricultural runoff laden with chemicals (synthetic fertilizers and pesticides) and nutrients is suspected as a major culprit responsible for many 'dead zones' in both inland and marine waters, affecting an estimated 173,000 miles of US waterways."[45] These environmental wastelands can be enormous. According to the National Oceanic and Atmospheric Administration, in 2019 the annual Gulf of Mexico dead zone covered approximately 6,952 square miles.[46]

In the United States it's estimated that farmed animals produce around 500 million tons of manure a year.[47] That's a lot of bullsh*t, and it's a huge problem. All that waste needs to go somewhere, and it does, often contaminating groundwater through nitrate and pathogens leaching from manure storage facilities and fields. Excess nutrients from high doses of manure "threaten soil fertility owing to unbalanced or even noxious nutrient concentrations."[48]

Up to Us

The world's anemic response to global warming reminds me of a story I first heard on the TV show *The West Wing*. You might already know it, but it seems apropos:

> A man lives in a valley, and at the end of the valley is a huge dam holding up an enormous reservoir. One day the man hears a message on the radio. The dam is about to break. All residents should flee the area at once. The man stays, declaring, "I'm a man of faith. God will save me." Sure enough, the next day the dam breaks, and the waters of the reservoir come crashing through the valley. With the rapidly rising waters about to reach his porch, a boat comes by, the passengers beckoning him to get in. "I'm a man of faith," he says, "God will save me." As the waters continue to rise and he makes his way to the roof, a helicopter appears, hovering above him and dropping a ladder. "Climb up," they say, "and we'll take you to safety." "I'm a man of faith," he replies, "God will save me."
>
> The next day, after drowning, the man finds himself before God. "God," he complains, "I had

faith in you. Why didn't you save me?" God looks at him quizzically. "I sent you a radio call, a boat, and a helicopter. What more did you want me to do!"

When I was considering going vegetarian for ethical reasons, it was a binary choice. I would or I wouldn't. Most of our environmental decisions are not as clear cut. We can minimize our impact, but we can't eliminate it. Being alive necessitates using resources. Some footprint is unavoidable. As a practical matter, you have to drive—or at least take a bus or subway. I try to not buy any plastic, but it is ubiquitous. When it comes to animal agriculture, you *can* completely remove yourself. Unlike other activities with environmental ramifications, you can stop contributing to the devastating impacts of meat with one simple decision—stop eating it.

The planet is letting us know in no uncertain terms that it's time to radically change our behavior—the scientists, the extreme weather events, and the record-breaking heat are our warnings. We are the man in the valley. It's up to us to save ourselves. *Cowspiracy* sums it up: every day, a person who eats a vegan diet saves 1,100 gallons of water, 45 pounds of grain, 30 square feet of forested land, 20 pounds of carbon dioxide, and one animal's life.[49] Each of us plays a part. The vegan environmental imperative has never been more urgent.

Chapter 3:

The Health Imperative

Tim is a freelance journalist and marketing communications expert. He moved to Berlin in 1988, the year before the wall fell, and ended up staying for nine years. During that time he went back and forth with vegetarianism, motivated primarily by concerns about how beings treat each other. Living in Germany as a Jew, he was acutely aware of the Holocaust and how Jews were considered lesser beings during the war. After visiting Auschwitz, site of the most infamous concentration camp, where nearly a million Jews were killed, he went vegetarian for the final three years of his stay. Soon after moving back to California, working in a high-pressure job, Tim noticed he was often getting cold—particularly his feet—sitting in offices. He thought eating meat might improve his circulation, so he started eating a little:

> *For years I was eating meat maybe once a week.... I was eating plenty of cheese, and I found it was hard to control my weight even though I'm fairly athletic—I run. At times I would eat more than I should, and when you're eating more than you should and you're eating meat and/or dairy, at least for me, my body heats up. And if I do that around the dinner hour or later, I really don't sleep, because I go to bed and my body is heated up, so I would not have many or any blankets on. When that would happen—which might have been maybe once every week and a half or two weeks—at three in the*

morning I would be cold because the food would be digested and I'd wake up. So that was really uncomfortable.

I clung to that temptation for many years.... I yielded to the temptation of overeating, or eating to the point of just feeling uncomfortable.... and if I ever had something that would throw my exercise regime off—I had a cold or I was injured for a month or so—I would gain weight because I wasn't exercising. And so in terms of not only health but vanity, I noticed that my lifestyle didn't quite make a lot of sense because it wasn't sustainable in a way it should be.

In November 2019, during a routine checkup, Tim discovered that his "bad" cholesterol was too high. With a family history of high blood pressure and heart disease, he was concerned. He decided to do something about it:

So I just said screw this. I'm going to go pretty much cold turkey vegan.... I want to bring my cholesterol level down to normal levels. I never want to think or worry about that again. So that was the catalyst.

Tim talks about other health benefits besides low cholesterol:

Then there are the fringe benefits I absolutely didn't expect. When I was a vegetarian in Berlin I lost weight, but I kind of forgot about that. I've never been radically overweight, but I noticed I'd grown out of some of my pants and I had to have some let out.... Now, without even trying, I'm back at my high school physique and weight.... From a health point of view I think it's terrific, and from a vanity point of view it's terrific....

And there is a slew of other conveniences. I don't really overeat that much anymore.... If I ever do overeat, what am I overeating? Tofu and wheat berries. When I overate on Thanksgiving—most people overeat over Thanksgiving—what did I overeat on? Brussels sprouts and maybe a few potatoes.... I certainly never have that terrible feeling of going to bed all heated up because you've overeaten and then waking up at 3 in the morning because you're cold.... So I sleep better....

For all those reasons, this has been one of the best things that's ever happened to me. It's allowed me to have a stabilized weight, allowed me to sleep better, I don't feel uncomfortable from overeating, my health is clearly better, and psychologically I don't focus on food as some kind of psychological comfort that I think that I used to. Food gives me nutrition, and I enjoy it. I like the taste of what I have, but I no longer yearn for eating those sweets or all that fat or all that cheese or all that meat. So I have a different relationship to food. It's no longer a crutch.

Tim is confident he'll never go back to eating meat or dairy and is very happy with a relatively simple vegan diet.

*

There are three main reasons people become vegan—morality, environment, and health. I began as an ethical vegetarian but noticed something over the years: when I eat healthier, I feel better. For me, the fact that a vegan diet is particularly healthy is not the incentive, but it's certainly an added benefit.

For many, including world-class athletes, health is the main motivation. Novak Djokovic is the world's best tennis player and one of the all-time greats. At age thirty-two he won the Australian Open in a grueling five-set match lasting four hours. For him, a vegan diet was life-altering:

> My diet hasn't just changed my game, it's changed my *life*—my wellbeing. And if I feel better, that obviously transfers to my professional life. Eating vegan makes me more aware of my body on the court … more alert. I removed toxins from my body, and with them went all the inflammation and other things that were messing with my energy levels. As an athlete, the most important thing is to keep your energy levels consistent—especially as a tennis player, where you're alone on the court for a best of five match. When playing for 3, 4, 5 hours straight, you need the right fuel … and for me the right fuel is plant-based.[50]

Carl Lewis, considered by many the greatest track and field athlete of all time, had his personal best times in his thirties—after going vegan.[51]

If you haven't seen the documentary *The Game Changers*, I highly recommend it. The film, which examines the physiology behind a plant-based diet, features vegan athletes like ultramarathon runner Scott Jurek, who won the Western States 100-mile Endurance Run seven straight times and ran the 2,200-mile

Appalachian trail in a record forty-six days. According to Jurek, "there was no question that a plant-based diet was fueling my victories." Patrik Baboumian, one of the strongest men in the world, got even stronger and bigger when he stopped eating meat, lifting 1,224 pounds to set an official world record. When asked how he was as strong as an ox without eating meat, Baboumian replied, "Have you ever seen an ox eating meat?"[52] The same can be said of many of the planet's strongest animals, including elephants, rhinoceroses, and hippopotamuses. The strongest primates, gorillas, eat a mostly plant-based diet. Tom Brady, seven-time Super Bowl champion considered by many the greatest football player of all time, and Venus Williams, winner of seven Grand Slam tennis championships, also benefit from a vegan diet.

I think about the vegan health imperative differently than the moral and environmental ones, where the obligation stems from your duty to others. Health is primarily about you. Bad health has incidental effects on healthcare resources and relationships, but ultimately you are the one who gains or loses the most from your food choices. Whether or not veganism is a health imperative is a much more personal determination.

There's a ton of material out there on vegan health. I'm providing an overview of a complex subject. The bottom line: there's no question a vegan diet is healthy, and there's strong reason to believe it's the healthiest.

The Healthiest Diet

In 2006 T. Colin Campbell and Thomas M. Campbell published a landmark book based on a twenty-year study of the diets of 6,500 people. The conclusions of *The China Study* are clear and startling: A vegan diet is significantly healthier than a meat-based one. Eating plant-based foods is associated with weight loss and lower cholesterol—Tim can attest to these—as well as greater longevity and lower blood pressure. It also reduces the risk of heart disease, cancer, diabetes, autoimmune diseases, Alzheimer's, osteoporosis, and other illnesses. The study found a direct connection between the consumption of meat and chronic disease.[53]

In 2018 the International Agency for Research on Cancer—part of the World Health Organization—published a comprehensive report based on over eight hundred studies evaluating the carcinogenicity of meat. It finds an increased risk of colorectal cancer associated with the consumption of red meat and processed meat and cites studies linking meat consumption to stomach cancer, pancreatic cancer, prostate cancer, breast cancer, and lung cancer.[54]

Other studies find that vegetarian diets may lower the risk of cancer generally,[55] prostate cancer (vegan diet),[56] colorectal cancer,[57] diabetes,[58] and heart disease.[59] A review of several studies finds reductions in cancer rates and other health benefits associated with a vegetarian diet, including "lower BMI values, lower prevalence of hypertension, lower prevalence of the metabolic syndrome, lower prevalence and incidence of diabetes mellitus, and lower all-cause mortality."[60]

In *The Game Changers,* Dr. Dean Ornish agrees: "People who eat a diet that's high in animal protein have a 75 percent increased risk of premature death from all causes and a 400 to 500 percent increased risk of death from most forms of cancer—prostate, breast, colon cancer—as well as type 2 diabetes."

Other advantages of plant-based foods are that they are anti-inflammatory, have low or no saturated fat (with some exceptions), and are high in fiber and antioxidants.

When I was in my early thirties, I shared an office with a health-conscious but omnivorous long-distance runner. One day, when we had the opportunity to have our cholesterol tested for free, he challenged me to a bet on whose was lower. I accepted, knowing that plants have *zero* cholesterol. Sure enough, the outcome wasn't close. I forget exactly what we bet on, but I'm sure it tasted good. If you're concerned about cholesterol, a vegan diet may be your solution.

Protein

When I decided to go vegetarian in 1977, my main question was whether I could get enough protein. This is by far the biggest health concern for people considering the transition to a vegetarian or vegan diet.

Protein performs a number of important functions in the human body. It's needed for growth, to break down food, and to make and repair muscles, tendons, ligaments, hair, and nails, among other processes. A person's protein needs vary depending on individual factors, including gender and weight. The USDA's recommended daily protein intake for the average woman is 46 grams and for the average man 56 grams.[61]

Back then I was reassured by *Diet for a Small Planet*, and today it is generally acknowledged that a vegan, plant-based diet easily meets our protein needs. Protein is made up of molecules known as amino acids. Of the twenty standard amino acids, nine are considered essential because the human body cannot manufacture them. Animal foods contain all nine essential amino acids and are considered "complete." Fear of protein deficiency stems from the fact that most plants are incomplete, lacking one or more of the essential amino acids. Fortunately, this can be remedied by combining plant foods to provide all nine essential amino acids. When Lappé wrote her book, it was thought that complementary foods must be combined within the same meal, requiring heightened vigilance. Today it is generally agreed—including by Lappé—that combining need not happen at each meal. Because of the way our bodies store and recycle amino acids, as long as you eat a varied diet throughout the day, your protein needs will be met.

Legumes, which include beans and peanuts, play a special role in a vegan diet. They are the best plant sources of the amino acid lysine, which is sometimes lacking in other plant foods, such as grains.

Many people mistakenly believe protein is the body's main source of energy. As explained in *The Game Changers*, this idea was first propounded in the 1800s by chemist Justus von Liebig, who posited that "vegetarians were theoretically incapable of prolonged exercise." Dr. James Loomis, team physician for the 2006 World Series champion St. Louis Cardinals and Super Bowl XXXIV champion St. Louis Rams, explains the error: "The actual energy for exercise comes mainly from carbohydrates in the form of glycogen which we store in our muscles. When we sacrifice those carbohydrate calories for protein calories in our diet, what ends up happening is, you will develop really chronic carbohydrate or glycogen depletion. And what does that lead to? Well, it leads to chronic fatigue and loss of stamina." By the time Liebig was proven wrong, his theory had already taken hold, influencing the USDA's first protein recommendations in the 1890s. The misconception persists today.

Vitamin B-12

It wasn't until well after I became vegan that I learned of perhaps the most important vegan health concern—vitamin B-12, which is essential for converting carbohydrate, fat, and protein into energy. It's also needed for DNA synthesis and the production of red blood cells in bone marrow and helps protect nerve fibers and rid the body of homocysteine, an amino acid that is implicated in heart disease.

The most common source of B-12 is meat and dairy products. It was once found in soils where food plants grew but has been depleted because of the widespread use of agrochemicals. It's also present in cultured foods like sauerkraut, kimchi, yogurt, and other pickled or fermented foods, but as a general rule it's the one nutrient often lacking in a plant-based diet.

It's important to be mindful of B-12, especially if you're over fifty, since your ability to extract B-12 from food may decline. B-12 deficiency can cause anemia, nerve damage, gastrointestinal disturbances, and elevated blood levels of homocysteine. Fortunately, we don't need that much, the body stores it for a long time, and it's easily obtainable from supplements—I take a multivitamin that has B-12 every few days. Many vegan foods you find at the grocery store, like nondairy milks and vegan meat substitutes, come fortified with B-12.

Calcium

Some people are worried about calcium, the most plentiful mineral in the human body, needed for building bones and keeping them healthy. Again, this is not an issue in a plant-based diet. Minerals originate in plants and soil, not animals, and a vegan diet can easily provide the optimal amounts of all essential minerals, including calcium.

Plant sources of calcium have additional benefits, tending to be high in potassium, vitamin C, and vitamin K, also important for bone health. It is believed the isoflavones in soy products—tofu, tempeh, soy milk—also benefit bones. While milk and cheese are promoted as good sources of calcium, they do not provide any more absorbable calcium than plant foods.

The best calcium sources are leafy green vegetables—kale, collards, mustard greens, turnip greens, Chinese (napa) cabbage, bok choy—broccoli, tofu made with calcium sulphate, soaked nuts and seeds, fortified nondairy milks and juices, almonds, almond butter, and sesame tahini. Spinach, chard, and beet greens have high levels of oxalates, which bind calcium, but are not reliable sources of it.

Craving

Jonna was born in Denmark and emigrated to the United States twenty-six years ago at the age of twenty-seven. After landing in California, she went vegetarian for three and a half years before falling off the proverbial wagon. She talks about her experience:

> *When I came to California from Denmark, I was blown away by the supply of food. I'd never seen a potato that wasn't just brown. I didn't know that potatoes came in pink or purple. I didn't know that leafy greens have flavor. The only kind of lettuce I was used to eating was iceberg lettuce. For lettuce in Denmark they use what we here refer to as Chinese cabbage. Those plants are very watery and have very little flavor. So that was the salad, the leafy greens, that I grew up with. So when I came here, oh god, mustard greens and all kinds of stuff. I jokingly say I became a health nut when I came to California. I started reading a lot of books about nutrition —* Diet for a Small Planet *and those types of books. I think that was very instrumental in me becoming vegetarian at the time.... I started taking a ton of supplements and eating an enormous amount of leafy greens and vegetables and stuff....*
>
> *[But] despite the fact that I put so much effort into ensuring I got all the right nutrients and supplements and stuff, I just wasn't feeling good. I struggled tremendously. I felt really lethargic and I didn't really feel like my brain was online.... And that was why I decided to start eating meat again....*

After about three and a half years, I ate a vegetarian Thanksgiving dinner, but the day after Thanksgiving I went to see a friend of mine. She was making sandwiches. "I know you're a vegetarian, but I hate to not offer. Would you like a sandwich?" I said, "Yeah, a turkey sandwich." She made me a turkey sandwich and I immediately felt better. It was just like, "Oh yeah, my body really needed this." It was very visual for me. I really felt like my body likes eating this. My body really needs these nutrients or whatever. So that was how I ended up starting to eat meat again....

It may very well have been psychological as well as physical. I think the mind-body connection is very strong. I felt a craving that I couldn't really ignore. Eating that sandwich was so incredibly satisfying. I felt energy that I hadn't been feeling for a long time. It felt like there was something missing. I wasn't healthy. I wasn't getting the nutrients I needed. With that little bit of meat I felt a lot better, a lot more satisfied, physically and mentally too.

Jonna's relapse is not unusual. Over the years I've talked to many people who say they tried going vegetarian or vegan but went back to eating meat or dairy for health reasons. Dr. Michael Klaper, a longtime advocate for a plant-based diet, explains the physical craving resulting from the unnaturally meat-centered diet many of us are raised on:

The folks who truly have a real meat craving and really desire it, I think it has to do with the food we eat as infants. When you think about it, at six months of age, when the baby is still nursing on the breast, with all the love in the parents' hearts, that jar of baby lamb, baby chicken, baby turkey is opened…. By age two or three they're in the fast-food restaurant eating their Happy Meals. They're off to an animal-based diet start.

And if you eat meat three times a day through infancy, childhood, through adolescence, puberty, through your teens, your twenties, your thirties, … you're going to get dependent upon the carnitine, creatine, the muscle-based nutrients that are coming in with the food. Your body makes them, but if they've been coming in pre-formed three times a day since infancy, what are your genes going to do? They're going to down-regulate their own production of carnitine and creatine….

Well, that works as long as you're still eating it—of course, you're brewing up a bunch of different diseases along with it—but if you suddenly then stop, … your body's still looking for those pre-formed nutrients. Now you have to make them all on your own.

Now, most people can gear up their genes and their enzymes to start synthesizing their own carnitine and creatine. But some folks might be a bit slower, might take six months or a year before they're really manufacturing that, and they get meat cravings, and when they eat meat and that pre-formed carnitine, creatine washes through their tissue, *Oh, I feel great. Vegan, shmegan, man. I'm a carnivore. I need my meat.*

And they do, but this is not normal human physiology. This is an acquired dependency created by feeding a human infant animal flesh three times a day.... No primate does that.... We didn't used to either. We used to raise our kids on oat gruels and things. Back throughout American history ... people lived on farms, and you may have had pot roast on Sunday and fish on Friday, but that was it. You ate out of your garden the rest of the week....

This flesh-based diet is just since World War II. We've been rich enough to indulge this, and so we've created all these generations of folks who are really dependent upon animal flesh, but this is not normal human physiology. I've seen three generations of children raised as vegans, and they turn into lean, healthy, bright people who don't have meat cravings. Their mouths don't water when they walk past a barbecue. These are healthy folks. They're physiologically different folks.

So I think what you're witnessing in these relapsed vegans are folks who had a very powerful meat dependency spawn and they're still having trouble getting past it.[62]

Another advocate of a plant-based diet, Dr. Neal Barnard, founder of Physicians Committee for Responsible Medicine, explains why animal-based cheese is so addictive. Dairy products contain casomorphins, tiny active compounds produced when the body breaks down milk proteins. Casomorphins attach to brain receptors and cause a calming effect similar to that of heroin or morphine.[63] Cheese is sometimes called "dairy crack" because it is the most concentrated source of casomorphins.

There is little doubt the craving people feel is real. The evidence also indicates that a proper vegan diet does supply *all* nutritional requirements. Whether there are some people who biologically *need* meat or dairy to be healthy is, like most things, up to each person to figure out for her- or himself. As a caveat, whom you consult is important. If you rely on conventional Western doctors, they are more likely to recommend meat. Fortunately, there are many doctors and other nutritional experts who recognize the benefits of a plant-based diet.

All of the Above

People who go vegan for one reason often come to appreciate all three. Tim went vegan for health reasons but sees virtue in each vegan imperative:

> *Although this isn't the major factor, for me there are moral issues that suddenly make sense in a way they didn't make sense before.... Obviously the environmental issue is a huge one. It certainly makes a lot of sense to not be eating anything that relates to meat or dairy from the point of view of environmental sustainability. It's great to show that I and other people can be very happy without doing that and that there's hope. If I can*

*do it and other people can, then there's actually hope for
our environment.*

*

The health benefits are substantial and reason enough to go vegan, but I urge you to always keep in mind the ethical considerations. I'll end this chapter with a health perspective from Nobel Prize–winning author Isaac Bashevis Singer: "I did not become a vegetarian for my health. I did it for the health of the chickens."

Chapter 4:

Speciesism

Syl recounts a formative incident from her childhood:

I was always very sensitive about animals as long as I can remember. In fact, I remember being maybe around seven years old, and I was helping my mother prepare dinner. She was rinsing off the chicken and I saw some brown stuff on the bone, and I asked, "What's this stuff?" She said, "That's blood." And I was like, "What?" "Yeah, it's a chicken." It was the first time it clicked in my head that the chicken we eat is the chicken that runs outside. I remember being very hard on myself for never having thought of this.

So I had my own little rebellion. I refused to eat any meat for dinner, which was a big deal in our family because we were ridiculously poor and you eat anything on your plate. I started to stuff my meat in my shoes and go to the bathroom so I could flush it down the toilet because I didn't want to eat it. And my parents caught me, and this created big drama in the house. My father didn't talk to me for almost two weeks, and then one day he came into my room and he had this book. When my father wanted to give us a lecture, he always pointed to philosophers: "Socrates thinks this, and that's how I know I'm right." He came into my room and silently gave me a book and left. It was Plutarch, and he had put a bookmark on a chapter about reasons for why you don't eat animals. It was his way of saying, "Okay, there are other weirdos like you."

After that, my parents made a deal with me: If you don't want to eat your meat, you give it to one of your sisters. Don't throw it out. When you go to college, you can eat whatever you want, but as long as you're in the house you can't throw out food. And so I patiently waited until I went to college, and I became vegetarian.

In 2011 Syl became good friends with a vegan she describes as a "moral exemplar." In large part because of his influence, and after reading more about it, she became vegan.

A paralegal with a masters in philosophy and several years' work on a PhD, Syl is close to her sister Aph and tells the story of her sister's transition to veganism and their collaboration:

When she started writing for blogs, I saw that she was quite a good writer, and I think she is very bright. I thought, "If only she could include the animal issue." She talks about race. She talks about gender. She didn't care much about the animal thing. So I took it upon myself—we Skyped all the time anyway—to make this person vegan. She needs to be vegan because I need her to write about animal stuff. So for months we were on Skype just talking about the animal issue. She and her husband, I was just talking with them and arguing and arguing, and eventually something clicked and they became vegan.

Soon after this Syl and Aph started a blog, eventually turning it into a book titled Aphro-ism.[64]

> *It's a collection of posts about several things.... I was mostly concerned there was a way that race was central in the animal issue that no one was talking about ... and so I introduced a view in which thinking about race would give us a new ground for an animal ethic.*

Speciesism Defined

Everyone knows the terms "sexism" and "racism." At the heart of society's relationship to animals is a word that may be unfamiliar to you—"speciesism." Speciesism is similar to other "isms" where one group is singled out based on some characteristic and afforded less rights. Singer identifies it as "a prejudice or attitude of bias in favor of the interest of members of one's own species and against those of members of other species."[65] In *The Dreaded Comparison: Human and Animal Slavery*, Marjorie Spiegel defines it as:

> 1. a belief that different species of animals are significantly different from one another in their capacities to feel pleasure and pain and live an autonomous existence, usually involving the idea that one's species has the right to rule and use others. 2. a policy of enforcing such asserted right. 3. a system of government and society based upon it.[66]

Speciesism entails a complete denial of rights for animals. The law classifies animals as property, reflecting society's wider treatment of them as objects. They are given some limited protections, but we can still kill them, separate them from their families, destroy their habitat, even experiment on them.

Oppression

Racism, sexism, and speciesism manifest differently but are grounded in the same principle and powered by a similar motivation. They are, each in their own way, *forms of oppression*.

> [A]s divergent as the cruelties and the supporting systems of oppression [of Black people and animals] may be, there are commonalities between them. They share the same basic essence, they are built around the same basic relationship—that between oppressor and oppressed.[67]

Racism oppresses by denying civil rights and abusing and demeaning people on the basis of skin color or background. The treatment of women throughout history as second-class citizens includes withholding such basic rights as property ownership and suffrage, placing them in positions of servitude, and, at its worst, subjecting them to physical and sexual assault. Speciesism not only rejects the possibility of rights for animals but affirmatively asserts the legitimacy of killing and eating them, simply because they belong to another species.

> Racists violate the principle of equality by giving
> greater weight to the interests of members of their
> own race.... Sexists violate the principle of equality
> by favoring the interests of their own sex. Simi-
> larly, speciesists allow the interests of their own
> species to override the greater interests of mem-
> bers of other species. The pattern is identical in
> each case.[68]

If you reject the notion of oppression in general, you oppose it in all its manifestations. It makes no sense to be against racism but support sexism. It's incongruous to grant rights to women but deny them to the LBGTQ community. *If you are opposed to racism, sexism, homophobia, or any other form of discrimination, it is incon-sistent to be a speciesist—it is inconsistent to eat meat.*

When we eat meat, we are engaging in an oppressive act. This is a difficult truth to accept. People never self-identify as oppres-sors. They are, in their minds, simply advancing their own inter-ests. But in speciesism just as in other forms of oppression, it is done at the expense of others. Speciesism, like racism and sexism, is a rationalization, not a justification.

*

Some people take offense at the analogy between racism and spe-ciesism, finding a comparison to animals insulting. To be clear, the equivalence is the presence of oppression, not the objects of the oppression. No one is denying differences between humans and animals. We suffer in ways exclusive to our species. For ex-ample, the loss of dignity is a uniquely human injury. But animals suffer from oppression in their own way, and it is suffering that unites all beings and renders irrelevant distinctions based on race, religion, gender, sexual orientation, or species. Oppression is oppression, regardless of its target.

This criticism is itself the product of a speciesist perspective. A comparison to animals is only offensive if you view animals pejoratively. There is no shame in being compared to animals. Most similes using animals are positive, not deprecatory. Wise as an owl. Sly as a fox. Strong as an ox. Free as a bird. Spiegel discusses this:

> Why is it an insult for anyone to be compared to an animal? In many cultures, such a comparison was an honor. In Native American cultures, for example, individuals adopted the names of admired animals, and had spirit guides—in animal form— who served both as teachers and escorts into the realms of the spirit world.... So how is that we find ourselves in a time when comparison to a non-human animal is instead hurled as an insult?...
>
> Comparing the suffering of animals to that of blacks (or any other oppressed group) is offensive only to the speciesist.[69]

Offense at the comparison stems from the historical ways humans have been analogized to animals with oppressive intent, a pattern discussed by social psychologist Scott Plous:

> With respect to speciesism, this reaction is an understandable result of historic attempts to portray human targets of prejudice as animal-like. African Americans have been depicted as apes, Jews as

vermin, women as prey, homosexuals as beasts, fat people as cows and pigs. Yet the very act of "treating people like animals" would lose its meaning if animals were treated well.[70]

Comparisons of speciesism to racism, sexism, and other isms are a reflection on oppression, not a commentary on humans and animals.

The Dreaded Comparison

In her foreword to *The Dreaded Comparison*, Alice Walker, winner of the Pulitzer Prize for her novel *The Color Purple*, writes, "Spiegel illustrates the similarities between the enslavement of black people (and by implication other enslaved peoples) and the enslavement of animals, past and present."[71] Among the conditions common to both forms of oppression examined in the book are ownership, lack of personal security and safety, destruction of the family, inhumane modes of transportation, vivisection, and secrecy. Photos and other images in *The Dreaded Comparison* are striking. Depictions of violence perpetrated against slaves and animals are stunningly similar and, when viewed next to each other, convey a powerful message of oppression's common bond.

Plous also notes comparisons:

> American slaves were often auctioned, branded, had their ears cropped, and were bred "like other live stock." Slaves were explicitly referred to as "stock" or "cattle," childbearing female slaves were called "breeders," children were referred to

as the "increase," and slave overseers were called "drivers." Field hands were frequently forced into labor with whips, collars, yokes, fetters, and chains, and they were often fed a corn meal diet (food thought sufficient for animals of burden). House servants, in some ways the counterpart of modern-day companion animals, were fed corn meal along with assorted table scraps such as un-wanted bones and fat.[72]

In making a comparison between slavery and animal oppression, Spiegel is not equating Black people with animals or slavery with our treatment of animals:

> [T]here are distinct social, political and economic factors which create and support the subjugation of animals, as well as differences between the possible manners in which blacks and animals could respond to their respective enslavements.[73]

But just as she does not equate, she cautions against the dangers of differentiating:

> That is why it is vital to link oppressions in our minds, to look for the common, shared aspects, and work against them as one, rather than prioritizing [certain] victims' suffering.... For when we prioritize we are in effect becoming one with the "master." We are deciding that one individual or group is more important than another, deciding

that one individual's pain is less important than that of the next.[74]

Walker discusses the implications of the comparison:

> It is a comparison that, even for those of us who recognize its validity, is a difficult one to face. Especially so if we are the descendants of slaves. Or of slave owners. Or of both. Especially so if we are also responsible in some way for the present treatment of animals.... In short, if we are complicit in their enslavement and destruction, which is to say if we are, at this juncture in history, master.[75]

Being Human

Some people reject the analogy between slavery, sexism, and speciesism on the grounds that slaves and women are, after all, humans. As humans, they have certain inalienable rights. While this distinction may seem relevant today, it was not to the oppressors of their time. The fact that slaves were people did not stop slavery. Slave owners focused on irrelevant characteristics to justify what we now consider a brutal, inhumane practice. The fact that women were people did not stop men from relegating them to a subservient role. On the contrary, men emphasized the difference in gender to rationalize their own behavior. A distinction based on species is equally arbitrary. "A line was arbitrarily drawn between white people and black people, a division that has since been rejected. But what of the line that has been drawn between human and non-human animals?"[76]

Syl takes an interest in the word "human," seeing it as more a social construct than a biological one:

> The idea of what a human is—the conception of human—really changed when westerners colonized the Americas. We know this because the first debate was about the humanity of the indigenous people there....
>
> If you're talking about racism, or if you're talking about sexism, what we're talking about is the exclusion of certain human beings from the general idea of a human, and in doing so, it justifies what would otherwise be considered to be a very cruel, inhumane treatment.... Some humans are not considered "real humans"—call it capital-H Human—whereas other humans will be capital-H Humans.... When we talk about Humans, we're not talking about a species. We're talking about this social idea.

Syl's current work involves reconciling what she sees as two conflicting notions:

> We have this idea that being human does have moral weight, and we believe there is something wrong when you exclude humans from the Human concept because of dehumanization.... To understand the badness of speciesism, the opposite may have to happen. You have to see the concept of the Human as being morally arbitrary.... You are literally using two contradictory concepts of Human.

Being Equal

In one of the great literary lines, from George Orwell's *Animal Farm*, head pig Napoleon declares, "All animals are equal, but some animals are more equal than others."* Critics of advocates for animals often impute to them the belief that animals are equal to humans and should be treated the same. I don't think in these terms and haven't heard any activist make this claim. Singer rejects this explicitly, writing, "a rejection of speciesism does not imply that all lives are of equal worth."[77] Regan's view is more complicated, distinguishing inherent value, which is equal, from other value, which is not. "[W]hile in my view all humans who satisfy the subject-of-a-life criterion have inherent value, and have it equally, it does not follow that the value of their life, any more than its quality, is equal."[78]

Treating animals with compassion does not entail giving them the same rights as humans. No one is suggesting that they vote or drive cars, just as no one is proposing that a five-year-old child vote or drive. It simply means affording whatever rights are relevant to their situation. At a minimum, it means not killing them, taking away their habitat, experimenting on them, or otherwise causing them to suffer.

---

* Orwell was inspired, in part, by animal oppression. "However," he wrote, "the actual details of the story did not come to me for some time until one day (I was then living in a small village) I saw a little boy, perhaps ten years old, driving a huge cart-horse along a narrow path, whipping it whenever it tried to turn. It struck me that if only such animals became aware of their strength we should have no power over them, and that men exploit animals in much the same way as the rich exploit the proletariat." (*The Collected Essays*, 3:458–9.)

A particular Buddhist teaching has always resonated with me. There are three types of conceit: the person who thinks he's better than others; the person who thinks he's worse than others; and the person who thinks he's equal to others. Among its meanings, this instruction rejects the very notion of drawing distinctions, which Buddhism considers delusion or ignorance. But we don't have to go this far to reject speciesism. *Veganism is not a choice between human rights and animal rights*. The choice is between causing suffering and not causing suffering, between compassion and indifference.

Intelligence

Many people cite intelligence as the defining characteristic setting us apart from other animals and justifying disparate treatment. Charles Darwin rejected that premise, writing, "The difference in mind between man and the higher animals, great as it is, certainly is one of degree and not of kind," and "There is no fundamental difference between man and the higher mammals in their mental faculties."[79]

Intelligence as a moral barometer leads to untoward results. The smarter you are, the more important and deserving of moral consideration you are—an inherently undemocratic notion. And the fact that some individual animals are smarter than some individual humans presents a quandary. Should these more intelligent animals be accorded greater rights than less intelligent humans?

Lex, a pilot for Southwest Airlines whom we'll meet in chapter seven, articulates a purported distinction between humans and animals propounded by René Descartes: "Some people would say humans have a soul [and] animals don't." The existence of a soul is, of course, one of the great philosophical/religious questions, and well beyond the scope of this book. But even if humans have a soul and animals do not, it's not clear how it follows that we may kill and eat them. They still suffer and desire to live.

*

Some people distinguish humans by attributing the capacity to act morally exclusively to them, rendering us "higher" beings. Like ownership of intelligence, this is a dubious assumption. Besides anecdotal stories of heroic dogs risking their lives to save humans, many studies have found "that some animals are indeed capable of behaving morally."[80] This does not appear to be a uniquely human attribute. This line of reasoning is, in fact, troubling. If the capacity to act morally is the criterion for moral consideration and animals lack this capacity, it gives us license to do anything we want to them—kill them, beat them, experiment on them—with no moral constraints.

*

This brings us back to the question of why we treat other beings with compassion. Is it intelligence? The ability to communicate? Skin color? Gender? Religion? It's none of these. They are all morally irrelevant. We extend compassion because of one characteristic—*the capacity to suffer*. There's an oft-cited quote by renowned utilitarian Jeremy Bentham that sums up the basis for moral consideration. I hesitate to use it because he wasn't a vegetarian, but it makes the point. "The question is not, Can they *reason*? Nor Can they *talk*? But, Can they *suffer*?"[81]

It is the nature of oppression to seek out any sort of difference, however meaningless, to hang its hat on, usually a characteristic over which the oppressed group has no control. When we seize on species to justify our mistreatment of animals, we engage in the same behavior as all oppressors, past and present. We single out a morally irrelevant feature, classify the group as other, and use this otherness as the basis for our oppression.

Anthropocentrism

Anthropocentrism is the belief or attitude that humans are the center of the universe, that we are the most important beings, morally or otherwise. Those who challenge this entrenched societal view are often vilified. When Galileo defended Copernicus's discovery that the earth revolves around the sun, he was tried by the Inquisition and found guilty of heresy. This theory—now accepted as scientific fact—threatened the anthropocentric world-view of the powers that be.

I have proposed that differences between humans and animals commonly relied upon to justify eating meat are morally irrelevant. Even if we are somehow superior to animals, it does not follow that we can kill and eat them. This is a minority position. For most people, the fact of being human is justification. Eve, whom we will meet in chapter nine, articulates this point of view:

> *I just don't value—it's a horrible thing—I don't focus on their lives as something in the hierarchy of things I care about. Animals are not people. Animals are not human beings.... I don't value animals the way I value human beings. I just don't. Because I'm a human being.*

I don't view animals as being equal, their lives as being as important as human beings' lives. I just don't…. I don't see them as being equal to the human species. I know they have feelings, and I know they have intelligence. I would never want to eat a porpoise or an elephant. I guess I don't view, for example, cows as being of the same value.

Human primacy is a difficult bias to overcome. My hope is that our species moves toward a more inclusive ethos, as described by Spiegel:

> The more we learn about the earth's environment, its ecosystems, and the creatures who live here, the more we see the absurdity in the concept of ranking species against one another. All life on earth is inextricably bound together in a web of mutual interdependence. Within that web, each species of animal has a niche for which it is more or less adapted, and attributes which others lack. It is only an anthropocentric world view which makes qualities possessed by humans to be those by which all other species are measured.[82]

The Arc of History

Imagine being born in a different place or time. What if you were a samurai warrior in feudal Japan, or a student at Plato's academy in ancient Greece, sharing ideas with some of the great philosophical minds of history? Perhaps you were born a prince or princess in eighteenth-century

Europe or groomed to be a king or queen in Africa. What would you be like? What values would you hold? Would you believe in democracy? In freedom? In human rights? In God?

This book challenges you to evaluate one of society's core beliefs—that eating meat is okay. A thorough examination of this tenet includes a sociological perspective and historical context. However strongly society and its members hold their views, values change over time. Slavery in the United States, whose vestiges remain, was abolished only 156 years ago. It was clung to tenaciously by an entire region of the country and done away with only by the most violent war in American history. Just twenty years before that war, both major political parties were proslavery. Today it is universally condemned.

The place of women in society has also undergone a profound transformation. We still have a way to go, but we're moving toward full equality in all aspects of life, from politics to the courts to the boardroom to the home. It's easy to forget that women attained suffrage a mere hundred years ago. Before then, ours was a country ruled completely by men.

When I read history, however well written and evocative, it seems somewhat abstract. Even film doesn't fully capture the emotional intensity of the times. The concerns of historical figures seem trivial compared with what we're experiencing in the here and now, less urgent and significant. Yet the people of bygone times were just as passionate about their lives and confident in their beliefs as we are. We regard the Greek gods as amusing mythology, but the ancient Greeks took them quite seriously, with the same faith and fervor we have in our religions.

Historical context gives us pause about clinging too tightly to present-day mores. As strongly held as they are, societal viewpoints invariably change and evolve. With this understanding, rather than simply accept norms, we can question them and decide for ourselves if they are consistent with the core values of compassion, kindness, and generosity—with wisdom. If they are not, we can reject them. The changing nature of societal norms and beliefs leads to one conclusion: *just because society says it's okay to eat meat doesn't mean it's okay.*

My thesis in this book is that when it comes to animals, society is getting it wrong. Morality is ever evolving, continually expanding its compassion and inclusiveness. Just as our views on slavery and women's place in society have shifted 180 degrees, I believe our relationship to animals will experience a similar seismic shift. When that happens, veganism will be the norm and not the exception. Ethologist Richard Dawkins makes a similar prediction. "In 100 or 200 years' time, we may look back on the way we treated animals today as something like we today look back on the way our forefathers treated slaves."[83] In evaluating your own conduct, I ask that you pose this simple question: *Are compassion and kindness consistent with killing and the animal suffering inherent in eating meat?* Hard as it is, I ask you to try to disregard the weight of contemporary societal norms as you consider this indispensable inquiry.

Abolition and suffrage started with the voices of a few, willing to question society's foundational values. The success of each movement depended on convincing others to join the cause, making the collective voice louder and more far-reaching. That's how fundamental change occurs—one person at a time until it reaches a tipping point. We don't have to wait a hundred years for society to be vegan. Each of us can agree here and now on a new ethic toward our fellow creatures, based on compassion and freedom rather than cruelty and domination. You can't change the world all by yourself, but you can make a difference. Martin Luther King, Jr., famously said, "The arc of the moral universe is long, but it bends toward justice."* This vision of a more just and kind world is the basis of the vegan imperative.

---

* He was paraphrasing the abolitionist minister Theodore Parker.

Chapter 5:

Animal Law

The video was shocking. The ducks were restrained, twelve-inch tubes stuffed down their throats and a pound of food—10 percent of their body weight—pumped into their stomachs, an excruciating process causing respiratory distress, locomotive immobility, and anal hemorrhaging. The long metal pipes would occasionally puncture the ducks' esophagi, causing them to drown in their own blood, or they would regurgitate, which they are not physiologically equipped to do, and then suffocate on their own regurgitation. Rats could be seen eating the anuses of the ducks, who were too weak and overweight to defend themselves. Force-fed three times a day for three weeks, the ducks' livers swelled to twelve times their normal size, causing the disease hepatic lipidosis—or as connoisseurs of fine food call it, foie gras.

When the video ended, the young man who had brought it looked at me and asked, "Is there anything you can do?"

*

After a year as executive director of Vegan Action, having resuscitated the ailing nonprofit, it was time to move on, but I was unsure about my next step. During my time at Penn Law, Gary Francione, a dynamic teacher and prominent animal law attorney, was a professor there. As fellow vegans, we naturally connected, leading to an independent study in that specialty. The reasons I had quit law remained, but the evolving field of animal law offered the opportunity to effect some real change. I took the

California bar exam to give myself options and when I passed decided to give it a shot. Fortunately Krissi Vandenberg, a very competent and dedicated volunteer, was ready to take over, so Vegan Action was in good hands.* With that, I rented a tiny office in downtown Berkeley, hung a shingle, and became an animal law attorney.

At the time, animal law was in its infancy, but I was not alone. Bruce Wagman, one of the great animal law pioneers, had the ideal set-up. Working for a big firm, he had all the accompanying resources and could devote himself exclusively to animal law. Still practicing, Bruce also finds time to teach animal law at three San Francisco Bay Area law schools and is co-editor of the text-book *Animal Law: Cases and Materials*. The Animal Legal Defense Fund, now a sizeable organization but then relatively small, was also local.

Besides the inherent challenges of entering an uncharted field, I soon discovered that civil law is a horse of a different color. Public defenders spend most of their time in court. Civil litigation is the exact opposite. It's primarily paperwork — written pleadings like complaints and motions governed by a voluminous set of state and local rules. Most lawyers learn the ropes as associates in firms, but I didn't have that luxury. I was thrown into the deep end and had to figure it out on my own as I went along. If it wasn't for the help of sympathetic lawyers like Baron Miller, a solo prac-titioner in an unrelated field who generously answered my many procedural questions, the learning curve might have been too steep to climb.

---

* Krissi still heads the organization and has done an excellent job popularizing the "certified vegan" logo, now used on over 10,000 products.

*

In many ways, animal law is a reflection of society's contradictory attitude toward animals. Under the law, animals are property/objects. If someone negligently drives his car over either your mailbox or your dog, the result is the same. You'll recover the money to replace the box or the dog and, except for veterinary expenses, nothing more. In California, animals have no worth apart from their replacement cost. The emotional component of the bond between you and your companion animal is not legally recognized.* On the other hand, laws such as anti-cruelty statutes and endangered species acts recognize that animals are more than mere objects—they suffer, have innate rights, and cannot be reduced to their market value.

I view animal law as the legal arm of the animal rights/welfare movement. The goal, apart from helping specific animals, is to facilitate and lead a larger societal transformation of our relationship to animals. As in other rights movements, like civil rights, the law can be an important tool. The following cases are representative of the range of issues I handled during my practice, a period filled with highs and lows.

Foie Gras

The plight of the ducks on the video was exactly why I had reentered law and encapsulated many of the challenges facing an animal law attorney. To initiate a lawsuit, a party needs standing

---

* Some jurisdictions allow for the recovery of damages related to your emotional attachment.

—the right to sue in the first place. Animals, as property or objects under the law, have no standing, so creativity is required.

Fortunately, California had enacted a statute known as the Unfair Competition Law (UCL), which prohibited a business from engaging in an "unlawful, unfair or fraudulent business practice." The UCL allowed any consumer to bring suit, so we had automatic standing. In 2004 California passed Proposition 64, a ballot initiative supported by business interests, which amended the law to limit standing to people who "suffered injury in fact," i.e., were financially impacted. This unfortunate change makes it much harder for animal rights, environmental, consumer protection, and other public interest activists to bring suit.

The principle of standing creates a potentially unique ethical dilemma. A lawyer's primary obligation is to protect his or her client's interests. Legally, my client was the human or organization bringing the suit. Per conventional legal ethics, my fiduciary duty was to that human. But as I saw it, my client was the animal. That's whose interest I was protecting. That's why I became an animal law attorney. It is a defect of the law that animals do not have legal standing and cannot be named as plaintiffs. My goal as an animal law attorney was to remedy that failing, not be bound by it.

Since the people who hired me were also acting on behalf of the animal, a conflict never arose between my legal human client and my actual animal client. It could have, and in choosing the interests of the animal over those of the human, I would have risked my law license. The legal establishment would have considered it to be a blatant violation of an inviolate fiduciary duty.

Standing is the first hurdle. A lawsuit also needs a cause or causes of action—the legal theory on which the case is based.

Causes of action are created by statute or common law—principles established in published legal opinions by appellate courts. Once again the UCL solved our problem. Violation of a criminal law is, per se, an unlawful practice, and we had a strong case that force-feeding ducks violated several anti-cruelty statutes. The UCL allowed us to enjoin, or stop, that criminal behavior.

Animals, of course, have no money. I, on the other hand, had to eke out a living, so I called Dr. Elliot Katz, founder of In Defense of Animals (IDA), a local nonprofit, whom I knew from my work with Vegan Action. The case was a good fit for them—important and potentially high-profile—and he agreed to finance the case. IDA and the Animal Protection and Rescue League were plaintiffs. Corey Evans, another animal law attorney, joined as co-counsel. We were good to go.

As it turned out, the case ended quickly. Sonoma Foie Gras, the defendant, was one of the few foie gras producers in the country. After they tried unsuccessfully to move the case out of liberal Sonoma County, there was a surprise development. I'm not sure why—perhaps the moral turpitude of their livelihood weighed on them—but the defendants agreed to close up shop. More significantly, the California legislature got directly involved. With all interested parties agreeing, the case was settled and the legislature enacted laws banning the production and sale of foie gras in the state of California. The outcome could not have been better—a total victory. Subsequent legal challenges to the ban have failed, and this remains one of my most successful and satisfying cases.

Hera

Diane Whipple, a popular women's lacrosse coach, was returning home, her arms filled with grocery bags. Suddenly, out of the blue, a dog attacked her in the hallway of her apartment building. She fought for her life, but the animal was too strong and overpowered her. She was dead within seconds.

When the police arrived at the scene, the dog's guardians* immediately signed a release, and he was quickly put down. But there was another dog present at the scene whom the guardians adamantly claimed was not involved in the attack. Nevertheless, Hera was taken away, and within a few weeks the city held a "dangerous dog" hearing. Hera was found to be dangerous and ordered destroyed—a euphemism for killed. That's when I stepped in.

There are an estimated 4.5 million dog bites a year in this country. Most are minor, but some cause serious injuries and occasionally, as in this case, a tragic death. In California, if your dog is accused of biting a person or another animal and someone reports it to animal control or the police, it triggers a legal process with rules and procedures. That process is problematic.

The police can impound your dog immediately, but further action requires an administrative hearing. This benign name belies the gravity of the situation. It is akin to a trial, replete with witnesses, but lacks important procedural safeguards, and the hearing officer has wide discretion in imposing a penalty, including "destroying" your dog. I was usually contacted after this hearing, at which point the options are limited. Appeals are an uphill

---

* I prefer "guardian" to the commonly used term "owner," which implies an animal is property.

battle, during which your dog is held in isolated confinement. As a cautionary tale, if there is an allegation of biting against your dog, contact a lawyer specializing in these cases *immediately*.

When approached to represent Hera, I thought long and hard before taking the case. It was receiving national press, and the victim was well liked and evoked enormous sympathy. My intervention on Hera's behalf could give the false impression that I was indifferent to the victim's tragedy and valued dogs over humans, neither of which was true. But dangerous dog hearings were not mundane matters for me. I know the pain of losing a dog, and I view them as death-penalty cases, which I oppose for both humans and animals. This was an opportunity to raise awareness about an urgent issue that potentially affects the ninety million dogs in this country and the families that care for them.

After an interview with the guardian and an examination of the evidence, I was convinced Hera was innocent. More to the point, it was clear her hearing had been rushed and due process had been denied. It was a classic railroad. I took the case with the goal of a new, fair hearing.

The appeal—a writ of mandate seeking a new hearing on procedural grounds—was argued before three Superior Court judges, and in retrospect the outcome was inevitable. The law was plainly on my side. There had been clear, incontestable violations of the governing statutes. But the case was a front-page story, with the dog's guardians being tried for murder. Dog hearings are risky propositions for judges, who in California and many other states face re-election. If they release a dog that is later involved in another incident, it could end their judicial career. In a high-profile case like this, the legal arguments are irrelevant. Even a decision to simply allow a new hearing would have jeopardized their jobs. It's not a risk most judges are willing to take. We lost, and Hera was killed.

As it turned out, I never received any negative feedback, and Hera did have at least one supporter. During the case I developed a friendship with Anna, a woman living in San Francisco who visited Hera regularly and checked in with me periodically to hear the status of the case. I suspect the outcome was harder for her than anyone else.

The Cow Palace

Alfredo Kuba was the consummate animal rights activist. Totally committed to the cause, he had turned his car into a mobile marketing machine, a giant triangular display mounted on its roof and custom-made holders stocked with pamphlets attached to the doors. Alfredo called me one day after trying to protest the rodeo at the Cow Palace, a venue just south of San Francisco, but being confined to three "free expression zones" far from the facility's entrance. Could I help?

This was a classic First Amendment case, and I liked our chances. The facts and law seemed favorable, I could file in federal court, which was less susceptible to political pressures, and it didn't pit animal against human, a matchup that always favors the human.

Despite a good outcome, this was not to be my best effort. My mother was diagnosed with terminal cancer a few months into the case. I was distracted and ended up moving back east to care for her during her final months, which coincided with some important filing deadlines. I remember the opposing attorney urgently calling me about a deadline the morning of the day she died. The judge was disproportionately angry with me for missing an earlier filing date, even though the rules were ambiguous, as they often are. She felt personally disrespected, and it impacted her judgment. Despite having a liberal reputation, she found no constitutional violation and dismissed the case in summary judgment.*

In a unanimous decision, the Ninth Circuit Court of Appeals reversed her decision, granting summary judgment in our favor. We won. Alfredo was able to protest where he wanted to, and the case established an important legal precedent for animal rights protestors at other locales.

The case was also financially lucrative. The law allows recovery of attorney fees from the losing side in certain cases that benefit the public at large, incentivizing public interest lawyers who could otherwise not afford to take on the risk. That rule applied here, so even though I took the case pro bono, I ended up getting paid by the State of California, owner of the Cow Palace. As a bonus, hours were billed at the market rate rather than my highly discounted animal law rate, so I was the recipient of a much-appreciated financial shot in the arm.

Adidas

"It is unlawful to import into this state for commercial purposes, to possess with intent to sell, or to sell within the state, the dead body, or a part or product thereof, of a polar bear, leopard, ocelot, tiger, cheetah, jaguar, sable antelope, wolf (Canis lupus), zebra, whale, cobra, python, sea

---

* Summary judgment is when there is no dispute over the evidence, allowing the courts to decide a case on the legal merits without the need for a trial.

turtle, colobus monkey, kangaroo, vicuna, sea otter, free-roaming feral horse, dolphin or porpoise (Delphinidae), Spanish lynx, or elephant."

In an effort to protect endangered species, California makes it a crime to sell the body parts of certain animals, including kangaroos. Adidas was marketing soccer shoes made with kangaroo leather, a clear violation of the law. The UCL afforded standing and a cause of action, so I filed suit with Viva! International Voice for Animals and activist Jerold Friedman as plaintiffs.

A lawyer who heard about this case summed it up perfectly: "It's a clear winner. But you're going to lose." He was half right. He understood that when animal welfare is pitted against powerful commercial interests, the odds are stacked against the animals. Sure enough, when Adidas made a clever but wholly meritless argument that the state law was preempted by the federal Endangered Species Act, the trial court agreed and granted summary judgment in its favor.

This ruling coincided with the winding down of my practice. It looked like the end of the road until attorney Orly Degani took an interest in the case and agreed to handle the appeal. The Court of Appeal agreed with the trial court, but the California Supreme Court was not fooled by Adidas's argument. It ruled in our favor —unanimously.

The story wasn't over, though. Shortly after this ruling, Adidas lobbied the state legislature, which removed kangaroos from the endangered species list, effectively negating the Supreme Court ruling and allowing Adidas to resume selling its shoes. The saga continued, however, as kangaroos were put back on the list in 2016 and remain there today, hopefully for good.

---

* California Penal Code section 653o(a).

This case involved a classic intersection of animals, law, business, and politics.

Vivisection

The pregnant beagles didn't understand what was happening to them. Isolated in a cold, sterile, research lab, they were injected with tumor cells aimed at the legs of the fetal pups gestating in their bodies. When their pups were born, the tumors from their legs were to be implanted in their brains, creating brain tumors for study and research. These beagle pups were to spend the entirety of their short, painful lives as lab animals, all in the name of human scientific advancement.

When Pat Haight told me about the experiments being performed at the Barrow Neurological Institute in Arizona, I was disgusted and pessimistic. The endemic challenges of standing and cause of action, not to mention politics, are even more daunting in vivisection cases. She had a theory, though, and it could work. There was evidence the experimenter, Berens, had exaggerated claims to the National Institutes of Health in his grant application. We could sue under the False Claims Act, which provides standing. We ran the idea by Jeremy Friedman, an expert in the field, and he agreed. When IDA stepped in to help with the funding, I filed suit with Jeremy as co-counsel.

The federal judge assigned to the case was unusually hostile to our side, so the appellate court had to weigh in more than once. The case was still active when I ended my practice, but Jeremy agreed to see it through. Sadly, after seven years, we ended up losing on an obscure technicality.

Ever since the time of Descartes, whom we'll learn more about in chapter seven, humans have debated the ethics of animal experimentation. For me there is no question. It is morally indefensible, the worst form of animal abuse imaginable. This is a controversial, multifaceted topic not adequately addressed in a few lines, but from where I sit, vivisection is irreconcilably incompatible with compassion, kindness, and human decency.

The Rodeo

When I was twenty and living in Las Vegas, a friend of mine suggested we go to the rodeo. I said yes, not really thinking about it or knowing what I was getting into. I was horrified. Grown men were abusing animals for sport. While not as barbaric as bullfighting, it revealed a lack of humanity that shocked me. I left after ten minutes.

When Eric Mills, a local anti-rodeo activist, approached me about a lawsuit, I was certainly interested. For twenty years several local school districts, including San Francisco Unified, had been taking students—seven thousand annually—to the rodeo at the Cow Palace. The rodeo performance for students included six events—calf roping, bareback bronc riding, saddle bronc riding, bull riding, steer wrestling, and team roping. In calf roping, a frightened calf is prompted into the arena by twisting his tail, raking his tail painfully over the slats of the chute, or slapping him. A "cowboy" on horseback pursues the calf, lassoes a rope around his neck, throws him to the ground, and ties his legs. When the rope tightens, it's common for the calf to abruptly jerk over backward and land on his back—a "jerk-down"—incurring pain, severe injury, even death. Steer wrestling and team roping also involve violently bringing an animal to the ground. Animals often sustain broken legs and backs at the rodeo, and at least seven animals had died from their injuries at the Cow Palace rodeo since 1982. At the 2000 rodeo a bull was killed in the presence of many children, leading to reports of nightmares.

As a legal basis for the case, Eric pointed me to a statute, California Education Code section 233.5, titled "Teaching of Kindness to Pets, Humane Treatment, etc." It requires that "each teacher shall endeavor to impress upon the minds of the pupils ... the promotion of ... the humane treatment of living creatures." Taking students to the rodeo promotes the inhumane treatment of animals, in apparent violation of the statute. I brought suit.

As a general rule, the single most determinative factor in a case is the judge, and here it was promising. The judge assigned to the case had a reputation as a liberal, a good sign when you're fighting for the underdog. But as it turned out, however liberal he was when it came to human rights, he was indifferent, even antagonistic, to this case involving animals.

A critical phase of a lawsuit is discovery, where the sides can question witnesses in sworn depositions and request written answers from each other. During the process, one of the teachers who had taken students to the rodeo testified he didn't realize what he was subjecting them to. He said it was "inhumane" and he would never do it again. Given the language of the statute, this evidence alone should have precluded summary judgment. Nevertheless, when the defendants made the motion, the judge disregarded fact and law and granted it.

The case almost garnered national attention. I was scheduled to appear on *The O'Reilly Factor*, the most popular show on cable news at the time, but was preempted at the last minute. Press coverage would certainly have changed the dynamics. Under scrutiny, the judge would have been forced to take it more seriously. The ruling came as I was ending my practice, and I couldn't find anyone to take it up on appeal, so the case ended unceremoniously.

Animal Law Today

My days as a litigator are over, but with so many talented young lawyers taking up the cause, animal law is in good hands. The field has grown by leaps and bounds over the past fifteen years. The Animal Legal Defense Fund now employs more than fifty people, including twenty-five lawyers. Most of the big animal organizations, like the Humane Society of the United States, staff a team of in-house lawyers. Animal law classes are commonplace in law schools, promising even greater mainstream acceptance when the current generation of students become judges and leaders in the legal community.

Closing Shop

In 2005 I faced another turning point. Over the past five years, I had laid the foundation for a successful, impactful career. But my hesitancy about re-entering law was well founded. I was moving away from confrontation, and the adversarial world of litigation was defined by it. Interacting with hostile opposing counsel, writing contentious briefs, arguing before—and sometimes with—judges, and trying to undermine the credibility of witnesses felt unhealthy. My duties as a trial lawyer impeded the development of personal qualities I was trying to cultivate—cooperation, understanding, and compassion. I appreciated law's emphasis on concise analytical reasoning, a skill I had spent my life developing, but I recognized my need for balance and a more heart-based approach to life. Plus, I just didn't *like* being a lawyer.

My meditation practice, started in 1998, had progressed steadily, culminating in a three-month silent retreat. It seemed like the right path for me, so I closed my law practice, left my girlfriend, and bought a one-way ticket to a monastery in Myanmar, where I stayed for two and a half months, leaving only because of health issues. After that, I moved from place to place, including extended periods in monasteries in Sri Lanka and the United States. While I'm currently engaged in the world, this remains my primary pursuit.*

*

My legal career had a common thread: challenging the system. From indigent people pitted against the full weight of the government to animals subjected to human cruelty and indifference to a malpractice case against a powerful law firm, I constantly went up against vested interests. When you do, it's always an uphill fight. People want to hold on to what they have.

The same can be said of veganism. It challenges the status quo, asking meat-eaters to relinquish something they cherish. Meat is the vested interest, and the vegan imperative asks you to voluntarily give it up for the sake of a disenfranchised group powerless to protect itself—animals, who are literally fighting for their lives.

---

* If you're interested in learning how to meditate, visit my website: www.vipassanameditationteacher.com.

Part Two:

Why Not Vegan?

Part Two Introduction

When Mike agreed going vegan was the right thing but added that he would still eat meat, it revived a question I've pondered for over forty years. In part one I discussed the why of veganism. I now turn my attention to the enigma: Why not vegan? Given the compelling moral, environmental, and health reasons to go vegan, why do people continue to eat meat?

Like many of life's questions, there is no simple answer. Human behavior is much too complicated for that. Each of us is the product of a multitude of complex internal psychological forces and external societal influences. To make an informed decision about our eating choices, the first step is awareness of these factors, many of which are hidden.

Some explanations in the chapters that follow may ring true for you, while others may fall flat. You might weigh the pros and cons and ultimately decide there is no vegan imperative. You may agree with the vegan imperative but, like Mike, continue to eat meat anyway. You may go vegan. Whatever conclusion you reach, I hope it will be made with greater mindfulness and self-reflection.

Chapter 6:

Cognitive Dissonance

For the past thirty years, besides raising five children, Julie has been working to ensure that students in her city's school district eat healthy, nutritious meals. While not trained as a nutritionist, she is unusually knowledgeable about the many facets of eating meat, from health to the treatment of farm animals to the environmental effects. Julie is very troubled by modern animal husbandry and thinks it is not fair to the animals or the planet. She is particularly concerned that we make our decisions around eating with consciousness and awareness.

Julie is not a vegetarian but is moving in that direction:

> *I choose to eat less meat. I choose to eat more plant-based. It's something that I'm working towards. Every once in a while bacon sounds good.... It's bacon and cheese and butter. I consider myself a vegetarian who falls off the wagon every once in a while.*

During the course of our conversation, I could sense Julie struggling with her answers. She recounts:

> *One of my daughters decided at seven years old to be vegetarian because the chickens they were eating used to be alive. I sympathize with that. I love animals and appreciate that, and beyond that, I've tried to help her find ways to complete her meals without meat. So that was a learning process. I appreciate it.*

Julie's daughter remains vegetarian twenty years later. When I ask Julie, who likes fish and shrimp, how she feels about a fish being killed so she can eat it, she responds, "You know, I have mixed emotions. I thought I would have been a lot like my daughter. It's convoluted."

At one point Julie good-naturedly remarks, "You're asking tough questions. Did you say I have to talk to you?" Though she was joking and happy to continue, many of the questions caused her obvious discomfort.

*

Once I made the connection between the food on my plate, the suffering of an animal, and my role in it, I faced a serious dilemma. I was a big meat-eater. I liked it. I didn't want to give it up. It didn't help that I had just returned from a five-week winter break consumed with meat-eating, which I'll describe in a minute. But I also place an extremely high value on morality, one reason I majored in philosophy (along with math) in college.

First identified in 1957 by Leon Festinger, cognitive dissonance is the uncomfortable emotional or psychological state that occurs when you have inconsistent attitudes about something or engage in behavior that is inconsistent with your beliefs. Cognitive dissonance arises all the time in our daily lives. You might be torn about exercising when you don't feel like it. An assistant might be uneasy having to lie on the phone about his boss's availability. If you fail to declare some income on your taxes, you might experience twinges of guilt. Smokers know how unhealthy it is yet continue to smoke.

These situations create internal conflict, so we employ strategies to resolve the tension. As Festinger describes it, the theory of cognitive dissonance "centers around the idea that if a person knows various things that are not psychologically consistent with one another, he will, in a variety of ways, try to make them more consistent."[84] One way to eliminate the dissonance is through the behavior. Even if you don't feel like it, you can summon the resolve to exercise.

When we're not willing to make a behavioral change, we utilize a variety of tools to make us feel better about ourselves. With white lies, society has our backs, condoning them and even condemning truth tellers. The word "white," which here means free from evil intent, gives cover by putting the liar's conscience at ease. A common justification for cheating on taxes is the notion that everyone does it. Smokers might convince themselves they're about to quit or understate the negative health consequences.

My predicament fit the classic definition: I wanted to eat meat. I believed eating meat was wrong. Something had to give.

Our attachment to meat is strong, and like any strong attachment, we don't give it up easily. Even though I was facing a moral dilemma, I wasn't ready to act. I'm not sure how long it took—a few days, maybe a week or two. In my heart I knew what I would do. It was more a question of getting psychologically prepared. When I was, I took the leap and went vegetarian.

The Meat-Paradox

Cognitive dissonance is unusually acute in the context of eating meat because of two powerful forces at odds with each other. Social psychologists Brock Bastian, Steve Loughnan, and Nick Haslam label this the "meat-paradox," defined as "the apparent psychological conflict between people's dietary preference for meat and their moral response to animal suffering."[85]

Most of us, on some level, are conflicted about eating meat. Bastian and Loughnan note, "A vast majority of meat-eaters also find animal suffering offensive, emotionally disturbing, and potentially disruptive to their dietary habits."[86] It was this cognitive dissonance that made Julie so uncomfortable during our interview. Her appreciation of both the suffering of farmed animals and the gravity of taking their lives gives her pause about eating meat. She relates a recent thought process:

> *I buy bacon maybe three or four times a year. I can live without it. I actually debated this the last time I went to the grocery store. Do I want bacon, do I not want bacon? I had this whole conversation with myself. And I went, "You know what, I've been under a lot of stress.... I'm going to give myself a treat."*

When it comes to the meat-paradox, since most people would rather not give up eating meat, they take measures—many of which are subconscious—to ease the tension. "When people are committed to morally questionable behavior, they will find ways to resolve dissonance to enable the effective pursuit of that behavior."[87] Before looking at some of these cognitive dissonance reduction strategies in the next chapter, let's take a closer look at the two incompatible sides of the meat-paradox.

Meat

Anna Rumatsky was the classic Jewish grandmother. A nurturing woman with a charismatic personality and huge heart, she expressed her love as so many do—through food. Her repertoire, reflecting her Eastern European upbringing, included such delicacies as stuffed cabbage, pot roast, fricassee, chicken soup, kasha varnishkes, and tzimmes.

The month before my fateful college conversation, I spent the extended winter break with my grandparents, who were living in a room overlooking the ocean in Miami Beach. Now a mecca for partygoers, back then this strip of art-deco architecture was a haven for octogenarians and up, anyone under seventy just a baby. With my grandmother devoting most of her waking hours to the singular task of making sure I didn't go hungry, it was a time of overindulgence and culinary rapaciousness. Every meal was some variety of steak, chicken, or hamburger. And unlike my mother, a reluctant cook, my grandmother erred on the side of excess. It was, in short, a gluttony of meats.

When I was a teenager, if you asked me why I liked meat so much, my answer would have been simple—meat tastes good. There is a biological basis for the attraction. Even though we think of meat as high in protein, what we actually crave is energy-dense fat, and the fat in meat is particularly appealing. Meat is also high in substances that cause umami taste, first identified in 1908 and considered one of the five basic tastes, along with sweet, salty, bitter, and sour. When meat is cooked, it goes through something called the Maillard reaction, which enhances the flavor and aroma and combines the substances in meat that cause umami to create a U-bomb—an intense manifestation of the savory umami taste. This combination of fat and umami is a powerful stimulus.

Many of the people I interviewed came back to taste. Julie mentions one of her favorite dishes: *"The one thing I do like is to take a jalapeño and put a piece of cheese in there and wrap it in bacon and put it on a grill. Gosh, it's wonderful.... It's delicious."* Jonna considered going vegan and tells why she decided against it: *"I didn't feel like I wanted to give up dairy, partly because I've been eating dairy my entire life and freaking love it."* The one thing stopping Emily from being 100 percent vegan is *"the taste of cow milk in my latte."*

But our desire for meat might be a little more complicated than just taste. Ori was raised vegetarian and is now vegan. When I asked if he ever craved meat, I was surprised by his quick response. *"Never!"* He found it "disgusting," comparing it to how most westerners would feel about eating a dog. He felt the same about the aroma, which many meat-eaters find so intoxicating. I understand his reaction to that unique scent. The smell of burning flesh wafting from a neighbor's barbecue evokes in me a confused mix of strong emotions. It reflexively triggers positive childhood associations with meat, but my brain just as instantly remembers it is not meat but rather an animal being cooked, and the same disgust felt by Ori quickly sets in.

Bernie, another longtime vegan we'll meet in the next chapter, also lost his desire for meat:

> I never had a great deal of difficulty giving up any of those animal products, particularly once I decided that they weren't right for me. Even today, when people ask me, "Don't you miss those things?" I usually say I don't see them as food, so they don't create any real temptation for me.

As we saw in chapter three, Dr. Klaper sees the desire for meat as the result of a dependency acquired from the inordinate amount of animal flesh we eat during our childhoods. It is this dependency rather than normal physiology that fuels our craving.

At least one school of thought holds that our desire for meat may not be biological at all. In *Why We Love Dogs, Eat Pigs, and Wear Cows*, Melanie Joy argues:

> Taste is cultural.... We like the foods we've learned we're supposed to like. Food, particularly animal food, is highly symbolic, and it is this symbolism, coupled with and reinforced by tradition, that is largely responsible for our food preferences.... Despite the fact that taste is largely acquired through culture, people around the world tend to view their preferences as rational and any deviation as offensive and disgusting. For instance, many people are disgusted at the thought of drinking milk that's been extracted from cows' udders. Others cannot fathom eating bacon, ham, beef, or chicken. ... When it comes to animal foods, all taste may be acquired taste.[88]

Joy coins the term "carnism" to refer to an invisible "belief system in which eating certain animals is considered ethical and appropriate." The system is invisible because the ideology is entrenched in society. It is our culture, not our innate biology, that determines what foods we enjoy.

*

In one of my favorite movies, a poor man in a small Russian village is thrilled to have the butcher — the richest person in town — propose to his daughter, despite the disparity in their ages and her utter lack of attraction to him. The man is happy knowing his daughter will be provided for. She, like me, is appalled. While fictional and anecdotal, this theme is based on the reality that in many societies meat is considered a sign of wealth and social prestige. In *Meathooked: The History and Science of Our 2.5-Million-Year Obsession with Meat*, Marta Zaraska asserts, "From the earliest days, meat was not just about nutrition. It was about politics and sex, too." Group hunting was a social activity, and collectively killing a big animal like a mammoth made the group feel stronger and more united. Zaraska compares bagging a large animal and sharing it with the tribe to winning the lottery and writing a big check for charity. "Studies show that in hunter-gather societies, able hunters attract younger and more hard-working wives and tend to have more children than less successful ones." For the Kulina tribe in Brazil, in a ritual called "order to get meat," the link is direct — meat is explicitly exchanged for sex.[89]

*

It comes as no surprise that eating meat is often associated with masculinity. Psychologist Hank Rothgerber discusses this traditional connection. During the perceived feminizing of the country at the turn of the twentieth century, eating meat was a way of resurrecting manhood. More recently, threats to hegemonic masculinity, including metrosexuality, increased the meat-as-masculinity discourse. The fast-food industry responded by promoting the notions that real men eat more meat and meat consumption restores masculinity. A study of *Men's Health* magazine found meat—particularly red meat—was associated with mascu-linity and meat-eating was identified as an attribute of the ideal man.[90] Another researcher notes, "Meat, particularly red meat, has been associated with masculinity and power, whereas fruits, veg-etables, and grains have generally been associated with femininity and weakness."[91]

As Arnold Schwarzenegger says to Sylvester Stallone during a scuffle in the movie *Escape Plan*, "You hit like a vegetarian,"[*] playing on the stereotype of vegetarian men as less manly than meat-eaters.[92]

Habit

From the moment I was born, I questioned things. I'm pretty sure the first word out of my mouth wasn't "Mommy" or "Daddy"—it was "Why." A high school classmate I recently ran into remem-bers me always challenging—respectfully—my teachers. In col-lege my favorite philosopher was David Hume, the great skeptic. Among his many contributions to the field, Hume posited that you can completely discard reasoning to explain human behavior. It all comes down to habit. "[T]he far greatest part of our reason-ings with all our actions and passions, can be derived from noth-ing but custom and habit."[93]

Habits develop over time as a result of repetitive behavior. In our society we're taught from an early age to eat meat and eat it often. For many it is the centerpiece of every meal, and most peo-ple never go a day without eating some meat. I prefer the term

---

[*] In real life Schwarzenegger, almost completely vegan (he eats eggs), is a big proponent of a plant-based diet.

"conditioning" to "habit." Our bodies and brains are programmed through conditioning to eat meat—and to like it.

A study looking at the relationship between eating meat and how people view animals examines the significance of habit. In her PhD thesis for the London School of Economics and Political Science, Carol Ann Norton writes, "Meat-eaters believe that they eat meat because they like its taste. However, the regression analysis predictor of overall attitudes towards eating meat turned out to be 'habit' alone. Habit is more behavioural in nature, where sheer repetition over years propels the behaviour's reproduction."[94]

Syl recognizes the power of habit:

> *Most people behave in quite habitual ways. This is the kind of system that we were born into.... It's just, that's what you do. You eat meat.*

As psychologist David Neal discusses, habits are hard to change:

> More generally, the pervasive effect of habits in everyday behavior is a key to understanding the difficulty people frequently experience in changing their behavior. People often fail in their attempts at changing everyday lifestyle habits such as their diet and level of exercise. Such failures are understandable given that cues such as time of day and location trigger repetition of past responses. Failures to change do not necessarily indicate poor willpower or insufficient understanding of health issues but instead the power of situations to trigger

past responses. Habits keep us doing what we have always done, despite our best intentions to act otherwise.[95]

Syl talks about this:

> It would be very hard to get people to question it, first of all. And that's not just with how we eat, that's with anything. And not even for ethical reasons having to do with the animal. If you tell them for their own health, "Listen, you're going to die, man, if you keep eating bacon or you keep eating all this unhealthy stuff," even when it comes to their own life, they won't stop doing it. Is it because they don't care about their life or they hate themselves? No, it's a habit.

*

Taste, social status, masculinity, and habit are just some of the reasons we are so drawn to meat. For Shelbie, a vegetarian we'll meet in chapters eight and ten, meat was once a comfort food: *"A lot of it is also comfort. When I was sad in college, I wanted something that reminded me of home, and I loved having a steak once in a while."* Whatever the factors, one thing is clear. People like meat and are, to varying extents, attached to it. This side of the meat-paradox equation is deeply entrenched.

Morality

Moral values vary among cultures and people, but one tenet of morality is almost universal—not hurting other people. Studies confirm that "prohibitions against harming others are among the most widely and deeply held moral beliefs."[96] Research also shows what you would guess to be true—the principle of not harming others extends beyond people. Virtually everyone cares about animal welfare.[97] Unless you hunt or fish, you probably don't intentionally hurt animals. For most of us, being kind to animals—treating them with compassion—is an essential part of being a morally good person.

We also differ in our relationship to morality and the role it plays in our lives. In 1980 the psychologist Augusto Blasi introduced the notion of moral identity, defined by one researcher as "the degree to which being a moral person is important to an individual's identity."[98] Moral identity and moral action are connected:

> Moral identity may be an important source of moral motivation; in fact, some argue that it could be the best predictor of moral actions and commitments.... Research has fairly consistently found moderately strong links between moral identity and action....
>
> [M]oral identity was linked to community service involvement and generative concern (a person's desires, commitments, and actions directed toward making a difference in the world).... Moral identity is associated with moral actions (e.g.,

donating money to charities and altruistic help-ing); moral emotions (e.g., guilt following behavior inconsistent with one's sense of morality); and concern for out-group members.[99]

Likewise:

> [T]here are both theoretical and empirical reasons to believe that the centrality of morality to self may be the single most powerful determiner of concordance between moral judgment and conduct.... People whose self-concept is organized around their moral beliefs are highly likely to translate those beliefs into action consistently throughout their lives.[100]

We can see how this concept plays a critical role in the cognitive dissonance of the meat-paradox, which involves a tension between your behavior (eating meat) and your morality (believing in kindness to animals). The greater the importance you place on morality, i.e., the higher your moral identity, the greater the tension. The greater the tension, the more likely you are to give up meat to release it. An estimated 4 percent of the population are sociopaths—people who have no conscience and don't experience guilt.[101] Being amoral, a sociopath experiences no tension around eating meat so has no reason to consider going vegan. On the opposite end of the spectrum, someone for whom morality is paramount is likely to give veganism serious consideration.

*

These notions bring us back to the riddle personified by my friend Mike. He has extremely high moral identity and in most areas of his life puts it into action. He is generous and honest and genuinely cares about the welfare of others. Not only is Mike familiar with the vegan imperative—he agrees with it. Yet he eats meat anyway. Our challenge is solving this puzzle.

Chapter 7:

Reducing the Tension

After graduating from high school, Lex attended the Air Force Academy and served fourteen years in the military. During the First Gulf War he was a fighter pilot, flying thirty-three combat missions during the forty-two-day operation, dropping bombs on the Republican Guard stationed just behind the front line and in retreat. He did not bomb any civilian targets.

After leaving the military, Lex became a pilot for Southwest Airlines, where he remains today. He is married with three children. His daughter, newly married to a former member of the Army National Guard, is a nurse. His oldest son is attending West Point, and his youngest son is still in high school. He loves dogs and has always had them.

When Lex was young, he hunted with a BB gun, shooting birds who attacked other birds, like blue jays. His attitude has changed:

> I noticed as I got older how I seemed to have more sympathy towards animals. As a kid I wouldn't think twice about hitting a bug or something like that. Now I'm finding a spider and I'm putting him on a piece of paper and throwing him outside, and I'm actually feeling bad about killing ants that are running around the house. I guess the mentality is if I don't need to kill, there's no reason to do it.

Lex talks about his diet and thoughts on eating meat:

> *I probably eat meat most lunches and dinners, with some periodic breakfasts.... As far as my eating habits, I never really thought much about meat being animals. It was just protein, vegetables, eat whatever I had. Still really don't think much about it....*
>
> *I generally don't think a lot about the food on my plate being an animal, but periodically I will. If people are having a discussion about it—usually it comes up in some sort of issue like obesity or when someone says why they're a vegetarian or why they're a vegan—that's when you really start thinking about it. No, I don't think too much about it. I wasn't raised in an environment where we talked a lot about it....*
>
> *People don't have a problem with eating meat because our whole society has been raised for most of human history eating meat and animals. It's just what we do.... I'm a product of society. I don't really have a problem with eating animals. I don't have a problem with farming animals for my food. That's just the way I've been brought up.*

Dissociation

The first step on my road to vegetarianism was recognizing something obvious but often ignored—the food on my plate was an animal. In our culture, it's easy to fail to make this connection, a psychological phenomenon known as dissociation. "Sufficient studies have now agreed that meat-eaters do not spontaneously connect animals to meat, and do not want the connection to be pointed out to them."[102] Jonna talks about this:

> *I remember back when I was vegetarian having reframed meat to dead animals. I think that's a shift, because a lot of times you eat a steak and don't see the cow that dies. But as a vegetarian it felt like I was not seeing it as just another food item.*

Society employs a number of strategies to downplay the fact, beginning with euphemistic or sanitizing language.[103] The word "meat" is particularly loaded. It objectifies the animal, just as some have used it—and in some circles still do—to objectify women. I remember one TV commercial that abandoned all pretense and subtlety, alternating the image of a sexy, alluring, scantily clad woman with a close-up of a big, juicy hamburger.

When I started writing this book, I had to make a decision: would I use the word "meat" or my standard phraseology, "eating animals"? While the phrase "eating animals" makes an important point, it turns off some people who might otherwise be receptive to the vegan message, so I settled on "meat." But for me it is not a pleasant word, and I remain uncomfortable saying or writing it.

We use words like "beef," "veal," and "pork" as euphemisms for the animals whose flesh they are—cows, calves, and pigs. Social psychologist Plous points out, "Even when the same word is used to indicate the consumed animal and live animal—as in chicken, turkey, shrimp, or lobster—the consumed animal is usually indicated by a singular noun without an article, whereas the live animal is represented by a plural noun or a singular noun with an article. People do not eat chickens; they eat *chicken*."[104] Animal slaughterers often use the word "harvesting," suggesting a benign process akin to reaping plants. At one point in our interview, Jonna referred to eating meat as "sacrificing" animals for nutrition.

At the beginning of *Animal Liberation*, Singer tells the story of visiting a woman who exclaimed that she loved animals. She talked about how her dog and two cats got on wonderfully and boasted of her friend who ran a small veterinary hospital. As they spoke, she took a bite of her ham sandwich. This is, of course, a common disconnect. Two-thirds of all U.S. households — almost 85 million homes — have at least one companion animal.[105] People certainly know how sensitive their animals are, and it's fair to say they would have to be pretty hungry before eating a cat or dog. But most don't think twice before sinking their teeth into a cow — in the form of a steak or hamburger.

One explanation for this phenomenon focuses on the word "food," where simply categorizing an animal this way has moral implications:

> Categorization plays a critical role in what is considered food and whether an animal falls in this category (or not) is socially defined. Different societies categorize specific animals as food or nonfood. For instance, dogs are considered food in parts of Korea and China…. We suggest that the category "food animal" may act as a conceptual frame or schema. Once an animal is categorized as "food," food relevant attributes should become more salient (e.g., tastiness, tenderness, flavor) and

food-irrelevant attributes less salient. Importantly, because suffering is unlikely to be considered food relevant, thinking of the animal as food may reduce its perceived capacity to suffer.

Categorization shapes the ways in which meat animals are perceived. People generally care about animals, however, when an animal is considered food its capacity to suffer is reduced, diminishing our moral concern.[106]

Given the importance of language in shaping our attitudes toward animals, many advocates put the word "nonhuman" before "animal" to make the point that humans are animals. I generally follow this practice but for simplicity's sake decided against it in this book.

*

By the time meat arrives at the supermarket or on our plate, it bears little resemblance to the animal it once was. It's no accident that meat is rarely sold with parts that would make its animal nature more obvious, such as eyes, ears, or tails, and processed meat is even less recognizable. Psychologists from the University of Oslo discuss this tactic:

> [Meat] processing often includes beheading, removal of entrails, flaying, or plucking and cutting the meat into pieces. It, hence, involves the removal of the typical animal characteristics from the meat, and the consumer is left with neatly packed, ready-to-cook pieces with none, or very few

reminders of the animal. This process gives people little reason to associate what they are buying and eating with a once living and breathing animal.[107]

University of Central Florida sociology professor Liz Grauerholz concurs:

> Disguising meat might involve presenting it in such a way that it no longer resembles any type of animal, allowing us to "experience meat and other animal products as distinctly separate from the animals that produced them ... because we do not encounter the animal until it is a sanitarily cellophaned package at a gleaming white supermarket."[108]

If you're like me, when you see a fish served at a restaurant with her eyeballs still in the sockets it's quite jarring. As a researcher explains, "The eyes particularly remind us of the animal's sentience, thus are potentially unsettling."[109] The sight of a whole pig roasting over the pit in a luau, often with an apple in its mouth, can likewise elicit a strong negative reaction. When study participants were shown pictures of pigs with and without their heads, "removal of the animal's head made [them] feel more willing to eat its meat and again this was due to an increase in dissociation and the drop in empathy it had caused."[110] Grauerholz's study of animal use in commercials is revealing:

> Most images coded in this study showed dead, cooked meat rather than live or illustrated animals. In these cases, animals were literally transformed

into meat, and there was virtually no resemblance
to any actual animal. In fact, images of meat—raw
or cooked—that do resemble the animal (e.g., with
ribs clearly visible) are the least common images
found. Camouflaging animals in this way is the ultimate in disassociation: consumers not only bear
no responsibility for killing animals for food, there
is little to remind them that their food or drink is
linked to an animal source.[111]

Dissociation can be the critical factor in people's food choices.
"The greatest difference between meat-eaters and vegetarians,
identified by a number of independent researchers, is that vegetarians, unlike meat-eaters, connect animals to meat. Meat-eaters
resist this connection even when prompted."[112]

Lex appreciates the importance of presentation:

*If I actually had to see where the ham came from—from
a pig—it would probably be a lot less appetizing. I get
it. We have certainly been very sanitized by where we
eat our food and how we eat it. If I grew up on a farm, it
probably wouldn't be such an issue because I'd be seeing
it on a regular basis. But since we have been growing up
where we're not actually seeing it—it's just presented
to us on our plates in a very attractive format—those
thoughts don't enter people's minds at all. Not mine.*

In some cases, the dissociation is complete. Julie, who works
on meals for public school students, observes, *"I have kids that I fed
in school who don't know where milk comes from. Milk comes from a*

gallon in the refrigerator. It comes in a box at school." As a former high school teacher, I'm not surprised.

*

Associating meat with the animal from which it comes has the opposite effect. Studies found that "visually reminding people that meat comes from live animals increases willingness to refrain from meat consumption, not only by increasing empathy for animals and disgust for meat … but also through increasing distress about one's meat consumption."[113]

Mike and I went to the same college and reconnected when I moved to Philadelphia for law school. Besides being friends, we're also business partners. A dermatologist, Mike is very entrepreneurial and has developed a new approach to treating irritable bowel syndrome.* Open-minded about his food choices, Mike describes two situations where association affects his eating:

> *Once in a while I'll try to make French onion soup, and I go to the meat counters at Reading Terminal Market and ask them for some marrow bones. They bring out these big femurs and start cutting them for me, and I get grossed out by it. When I start using them, I cook them and then I boil them. When the soup is the finished product, I don't really feel like eating it, because I know what went into it, whereas if I buy French onion soup at a restaurant, I love it. I don't like seeing a femur.*
>
> *If I go to a pig roast, I don't really enjoy that pig. I like a nice pulled-pork sandwich you get from Reading*

---

* www.IBS-80.com.

Terminal, but if I go to a pig roast for a graduation party with a pig with an apple in its mouth, I don't really want to eat that.

Syl tells a story about her personal connection to "food" animals when she was growing up:

We were so poor that it came to a point where going grocery shopping was almost impossible, so we started to just grow our own food. My father got a whole bunch of chickens, and he said, "They're going to grow up and they're going to be food," basically. We got a couple of rabbits. We grew vegetables and had fruit, and we became friends with the chickens. One day my father killed one, and I remember for dinner the chicken sitting there, and we all kind of just stared at it. Nobody would touch it. My mother said, "Okay, I'll just get you some oatmeal."

And then I remember my father crying for two weeks. I heard him from his bedroom door crying about it. So then he decided—the chicken was just sitting in the fridge the whole time—after that, we're going to have a funeral for this chicken. So we had a funeral, and from now on they're going to be our pets. We kept all these chickens, and they were just our friends. Same with the rabbits. He wouldn't kill the rabbits, and the rabbits became our friends. He eventually felt bad that they were enclosed in our property, and eventually he just let them go....

> *My father ended up buying twice as much chicken grain. He would give half of it to the chickens, and my mother would boil and season the rest for us. That's what we did until we were able to get more money to go to the store again. It turns out we didn't eat the chick-ens—we ate the chicken grain!*

She adds:

> *There's something about an animal living there and see-ing the animal as an actual living being versus the pack-aged form that makes a big difference.... Whether we package it so it doesn't look like an animal anymore, or instead of calling it a cow you call it beef, or even just the concept of food—talking about it as food, and sud-denly it's "Oh yeah, it's okay for me to treat the animal differently."*

One respondent to my survey wrote about becoming vege-tarian for six years after befriending a pig. Another became and remains vegetarian after she *"hit a deer on the road and vowed to her as she lay dying I would never eat meat again."*

*

Bernie is senior principal strategist for communications at the Humane Society of the United States. A historian, he wrote his dissertation on the history of the animal protection movement in the United States between 1866 and 1930. Bernie became vegetarian at the precocious age of three:

> *I was born in 1960. Sometime around late 1963 or early 1964, I was outside on our property feeding birds in the*

yard with my father and came in and noticed my mother putting a chicken into the oven whole. "What is that?" I asked. She replied, "That's a chicken." I said, "The chicken—a bird?" "Yeah, yeah, of course, of course." When the time came for dinner, I didn't want to eat it.

They let me get away with it, but then in the days afterward I continued to avoid eating animals and began to speak about it. My parents were very respectful of that. My parents were social activists driven by principles and respect for individual conscience and freedom of thought and action and so forth, and I think this shaped their response, which I always considered a great gift, because they recognized even in a child that it can become a matter of conscience. They didn't deceive me. If I could confirm that something was meat or derived from an animal, they confirmed it if I asked and pursued it. They didn't go out of their way to identify all those items and tell me to avoid them, but they didn't deceive me when I found my own way to it. By the time I was eight, I had eliminated just about everything in the way of meat products.... I had really figured out clearly what things were meat and derived from animals and what weren't. And so the last meat I had, at least knowingly, was at a Boy Scout Jamboree in 1968.

My mother, consistent with the basic respect they had shown for the choice, made one simple rule.... I had to eat everything else.... I couldn't avoid beets or peas or anything else on the table....

> *I think it was a good, rational way to handle a child's instinct. I've had friends who came to vegetarianism as children, or wanted to. Some were supported. I remember one father, however, telling me to his great shame that he had lied to his son and that this had haunted him for many, many years.... I had another friend whose parents forced her to sit at the kitchen table after she rejected the meat product and said, "You'll sit here until you finish." They found her the next day sleeping with her head on the kitchen table. These anecdotes made me grateful for the approach that prevailed in our home.*

Eventually, via different routes, Bernie's brother, sister, and parents became vegetarian:

> *Everyone in the family came to it in their own way by their own will. I think obviously our choices were reinforcing of one another's choices. But I really feel like I never propagandized in my own home. Other people found their own natural pathways to it, which is the way I think it ought to go.*

When Bernie was twenty-three, he attended an international vegetarian conference, where he was introduced to animal rights activists and exposed to a wide range of animal-related issues. He was particularly affected by the book **Animal Factories**.*

---

* This book by Peter Singer and Jim Mason was the most influential factor in my transition to veganism as well.

It brought a moral shock to me that I never experienced before, and it got me thinking that if you really think these things are wrong, you should get out there and start telling other people that they are wrong. Your own individual choice—a choice of conscience—while very good, is not enough given the scope of the problem and your deeper understanding. Over the next months I found myself falling in with the same kind of people that I met at the conference....

In my case veganism came a little more slowly. I began to read and look at some of the literature suggesting that dairy and eggs were responsible for greater suffering and other consequences than meat itself, and of course that was reinforced by getting involved in the grassroots animal rights movement.

*

It's common for children, usually between the ages of five and nine but as with Bernie sometimes younger or older, to have strong reactions when they realize the meat they're eating is actually an animal. In chapter four we saw this with Syl, whose reaction was similar to Bernie's. Since children intuitively don't want to hurt animals, eating meat creates cognitive dissonance even at that young age.

Tim tells the story of taking his five-year-old son fishing, something he did with his grandfather as a boy:

We took it into the cabin, and without thinking about it, here I am sawing off the head of the fish. Aaron says to me, "Couldn't we just put it into an aquarium?" I felt

absolutely devastated. It was like living in a nightmare.
I pan-fried it. I ate it. I don't know if he ate any of it. He
was so affected that we had some leftover earthworms
and he wanted to make sure they were put back into the
earth.... I'll never forget that. I also remember when he
found out—maybe about a year or two later—that the
lamb he was eating was some living being, and actually
it was from babies. He was absolutely beside himself. He
didn't become a vegetarian, but it was a real awakening
for him, and an outrage.

In the right environment with supportive parents, a child becomes vegetarian and stays that way, like Julie's daughter and Bernie. More often than not, the sentiment is not cultivated and the child is "socialized," taught that eating meat is normal and good despite his or her natural inclination.

As we saw with Tim's son, the prospect of eating a baby animal strikes a particularly sensitive nerve, a point noted in the study of animals in commercials:

> [T]hat baby animals are used so seldom to sell food
> products (though perhaps not non-food related
> products) suggests that marketers understand that
> the effect on consumers may be the opposite of
> what is desired. It is one thing to conceive of eating
> an adult animal but something entirely different to
> think about eating her babies. This may explain
> why not a single image advertised veal products.[114]

*

John Updike, author of the "Rabbit" series, captures the sentiment of dissociation, telling an interviewer, "I'm somewhat shy about the brutal facts of being a carnivore. I don't like meat to look like animals. I prefer it in the form of sausages, hamburgers and meat loaf, far removed from the living thing."[115]

Out of Sight, Out of Mind

It's a challenge for me to socialize when people are eating meat. When I see someone eating a hamburger or piece of chicken, I don't see food. I see an animal, and I feel its suffering. It's very real for me—every time! This hasn't diminished in the forty-plus years since I stopped eating meat. It's physically and emotionally distressing.

Humans are genetically wired to react most strongly to what is visual and before them. It's one thing to hear or read about something and quite another to witness it. Although we have the capability to think abstractly, being physically removed from an event severely weakens its emotional potency. Writing about moral disengagement, psychologist Albert Bandura explains, "It is easier to harm others when their suffering is not visible and when destructive actions are physically and temporally remote from their injurious effects.... When people can see and hear the suffering they cause, vicariously aroused distress and self-censure serve as self-restrainers."[116]

Slaughterhouses—a horror for both human and animal, hell on earth—are hidden from view for a reason. Invisibility enables us to disconnect the final product from the anguish and killing inherent in the process. As Bastian and Loughnan observe, "By making meat production distant from the consumer, people need not think about the path from paddock to plate."[117] Absent actually seeing this violence, the visceral impact of the connection between the sanitized product on our plate and the suffering of an animal is severely diminished. Norton notes:

> In the same way that "[t]elevised images of distant misery don't seem to belong to the same world as our familiar daily round" ... slaughterhouses and intensive farms are, for many people, abstract ideas: things that belong to other people in other places. They are unrelated to the hermetically sealed meat in smart packages on designer supermarket shelves.[118]

Lex has never been to a slaughterhouse or seen an animal slaughtered but appreciates the potential impact:

> *I think it would affect you in a negative way. Way back when, when everybody was raised on a farm, you saw slaughtered food so were desensitized. Today in America, unless you're raised on a farm, you don't see it. We don't buy our food hanging in a wet market where you see half of the animal hanging there. It's very wrapped up, it's very sanitized, so we're not really thinking a lot about it. For that reason we're probably not as desensitized to it. Most of the time when you deal with animals in this country, it is in the form of a pet or in the environment where they're all friendly and happy, so you don't really think about killing them and eating them.*

Yeah, I think it would definitely upset me and a lot of people if they actually saw a slaughterhouse.

It's not uncommon for people to become vegetarian after visiting a slaughterhouse. The Venerable Geshe Phelgye —affectionately known as Geshe-la—a Tibetan monk and former member of the Tibetan Parliament in Exile, was raised in a meat-eating culture. He went vegetarian after going to a slaughterhouse to buy some meat for a sick friend and described the experience in the film *Animals and the Buddha*:

> Normally people have no idea what animals go through. It is only realized when you get to see what actually happens in the slaughterhouses. Until then you wouldn't realize it. And then when you see it, you wonder if it is really appropriate to eat them.
>
> It's really horrifying. Certain slaughterhouses have all the animals that are supposed to be slaughtered for the day standing in the corner out there, and one by another they are slaughtered in front of the rest of the animals. You can imagine how terrifying that experience would be. Imagine yourself being out there and all your friends and colleagues being slaughtered and you are in the line.... I can't imagine there is something more horrifying and painful.
>
> ... It's just heartbreaking. So we need to actually see those things, how we humans are causing so much trouble to other fellow sentient beings.[119]

Mike's good friend Tim, an orthopedic surgeon, *"had to get some joints for laser research he was doing, so he went to a slaughterhouse to get these joints. He has not eaten beef since."* My sister became vegetarian after visiting a slaughterhouse during a vacation in Costa Rica. If you hesitate to do this in person, I recommend the excellent documentary *Glass Walls*, narrated by Paul McCartney, which you can find on YouTube.[120]

*

The nursery rhyme "Old MacDonald Had a Farm" and its catchy refrain "E-I-E-I-O" may evoke fond memories. It's a happy song. "With a moo moo here and a moo moo there, an oink oink here and an oink oink there, a quack quack here and a quack quack there, here a quack, there a quack, everywhere a quack quack." What could be more idyllic? The depiction of farmed animals as joyful and carefree in children's songs and books belies the grim reality of their lives. Classified by one website as educational materials,[121] these narratives counter cognitive dissonance by falsely depicting, and thereby hiding, the true nature of modern-day food farms.

Personal Responsibility

One of the key psychological steps for me in the transition to vegetarianism was recognizing that when I ate meat, I was an *accomplice* to the killing of an animal. There was a direct cause-and-effect relationship between my choice and the taking of a life. The invisibility and remoteness of the process could not alter this fact. Denying personal responsibility, on the other hand, serves to resolve cognitive dissonance. In its absence you are blameless, eliminating the guilt component of the meat-paradox.

With seven billion humans on earth and an estimated seventy billion animals killed annually for food, it's easy to downplay the significance of our individual impact to the point where we think it's meaningless. After all, the system will persist without you. What difference would it make if you stopped eating meat? Animals will be killed anyway.

I asked Eve if she feels that when she eats meat she is directly responsible for an animal being killed:

> No, because unless I were involved in really trying to convert more people to vegetarianism or veganism, it wouldn't make that much of a difference if I and my family stopped eating meat. It wouldn't move the needle. I know if everyone stopped, then less meat would be sold....
>
> I think that animal would be killed anyway. I really don't make that big a difference. I could make a little difference, but probably negligible.

I asked Julie whether it would make a difference if she gave up meat:

> Probably not right away. Probably not anything big.... If I felt like I was making a statement, nobody listens to one person. They listen to multiple voices. They listen to people they think know things.... But me, not buying bacon three or four times a year, ten dollars. That's not going to move the meter.

The consequences of our behaviors may be abstract or remote and may seem insignificant, but every one of our actions counts, however marginally. The meat market, like any, is controlled by the laws of supply and demand. When you buy meat, another animal is killed to replace it. Every time we eat meat, we perpetuate the killing. As Eve alluded to, the reverse is also true—by choosing to not eat meat, we reduce the demand and thus the killing. If you don't buy a chicken, in the long run one less chicken will be killed.

Looked at another way, if no one ate meat, no animals would be killed. They are killed only because there is a demand for meat. Every consumer of meat helps maintain the industry. If no one bought meat, there would be no meat industry. Not a single animal would be harmed.

I'm reminded of a story by Loren Eiseley:

> One day a man was walking along the beach when he noticed a boy picking up and gently throwing things into the ocean. Approaching the boy, he asked, "Young man, what are you doing?" The boy replied, "Throwing starfish back into the ocean. The surf is up and the tide is going out. If I don't throw them back, they'll die." The man laughed to himself and said, "Do you realize there are miles and miles of beach and hundreds of starfish? You can't make any difference." After listening politely, the boy bent down, picked up another starfish, and threw it into the surf. Then, smiling at the man, he said, "I made a difference to that one."[122]

The boy could have been disheartened and overwhelmed. He couldn't possibly save them all, so what difference would it make if he saved a few? It makes a big difference to those few. Even if you can't rescue them all, there is value in every life saved. And if other people happen to come along and join the effort, collectively you can save all the stranded animals.

The enormity of the killing in the meat industry does not change or negate the principle: *when we eat meat, we are personally responsible for the death of an animal.*

Jonna, who feels she needs to eat meat for health reasons, recognizes that she's contributing to the suffering of animals:

> *Probably to some degree, yes. I don't feel good about that at all. Not at all.... I don't feel like I have a lot of power there. I feel like I have to choose between being healthy — getting the nutrients that I want and need — and exposing animals to suffering. Absolutely. I wish it wasn't that way. I don't feel like I have any control over it. My power is to go out and choose products that at least seem to come from ethical businesses.*

Emily also acknowledges that every time she drinks milk, even a little, she is contributing to animal suffering. Her elaboration on this subject will be an important section in the next chapter.

It's true you alone cannot end the inhumanity of the meat and dairy industry. But you can refuse to be part of it. The consequence is real, and the cumulative effect can fundamentally transform the way the world feeds itself and treats animals.

*

The anonymity of the process is another way we deny personal responsibility. Some unknown person in a faraway place hidden from view does the dirty work. We pay others to slaughter so we can eat the hamburger or bacon. But we remain culpable. Even though we don't personally kill the animal, in soliciting the act *we are complicit*. From a moral perspective, there is no distinction between killing an animal yourself and having someone do it on your behalf, even anonymously.

The Buddhist "three purities" principle, discussed in chapter one—that you can eat an animal as long as it was not killed for you—is a variation of this thinking. This doctrine implies that if the animal was not killed for you specifically, you are not responsible for its death. This raises the question: When you buy meat at a market or restaurant, was the animal killed for you? Clearly the butcher did not have you in mind when slaughtering the animal, but this is a distinction without a difference. It was killed for the generic consumer—you. Whether or not the animal had your name on her, you solicited the act and bear personal responsibility.

The anonymity of the killing in the meat industry does not change or negate the principle: *when we eat meat, we are personally responsible for the killing of an animal.*

Tim has strong opinions about this:

> Going vegan ended a contradiction in my mind. I always knew there was something wrong with not being the person that was willing to kill something if I wanted to eat it.... There is something cowardly and very dangerous in terms of life in general in compartmentalizing unpleasant things that destroy or damage living beings

and then benefitting from that damage but not seeing it. Out of sight, out of mind. That's what happened during the Holocaust to a very large degree.... You don't witness the death and you don't participate in the death. I felt that I was part of something hypocritical. Since I've become vegan, I'm no longer part of that, and so I feel a lifting of an ethical contradiction that was inside me.

Eve discusses the notion of killing the animal yourself:

I think farms where people raise their own animals and then kill their own animals would be the optimal way to occasionally have meat. You're willing to actually take the life of something because you need to eat it.... That would be the optimal way in the best of all possible worlds to have meat, because the reality of the death and making sure that the animal was raised properly would be close to me and I would be conscious of it, versus what I do now, which is choose to not be conscious of the ways the cows are milked and the bad places, which are probably most of the places.

After expressing her concern for all living creatures, Julie talks about eating bacon:

I think it's because I'm not slaughtering the pig. Somebody else is doing it for me. If I was slaughtering the pig, I'd probably only do it once a year. If I was raising it, I'd be more conscious of it. If I went to my butcher and said, "This is the pig that I raised this year, and here's some bacon," that would make it more personal for me. That would be different.

Syl observes, *"I think if most people had to kill their food, they would begin to see the light."*

*

The dissonance reduction strategy of denying personal responsibility is summarized by ethicist Les Mitchell:

> Billions of consumers purchase nonhuman animal products, so it is difficult to assign any personal responsibility for the death of a calf to an individual who is purchasing a pack of burgers or a container of milk. Although, by their actions these consumers support the phenomenon of nonhuman farming, they are anonymous buyers of goods and so are themselves essentially *deindividuated*. A person may consider that many other people are doing the same thing as them, feeling that the meat industry will not stop because he or she, as an individual, fails to buy its products and also that the calf has, anyway, already been killed. In this way there is the potential for *displacement of responsibility* (I didn't ask anyone to do it), as well as *diffusion of responsibility* (other people buy these products, so it wasn't done for me personally, and it would happen anyway).[123]

Moderation

After my father's death I grew close to his brother, my uncle Sam. As a young man I spent many nights at his apartment in New York City, one of those below-ground units that you walk down to, the windows looking up incongruously at the legs of the passers-by. His home was filled with artifacts from all corners of the world, amassed over the course of a life-time of travels, and he was host to a constant stream of exotic foreign guests. Sam was a vegetarian — mostly. Every once in a while he couldn't resist a hot pastrami sandwich. We would argue. "Everything in moderation," he would say, not willing to let go of this last vestige of carnivorism.

For many human activities the question is how much is enough. What's the right balance? With the environment, however conscientious you are, you can always do more. You can cut back on driving and flying, buy less plastic, use less power. But even the most ardent environmentalist can only minimize his or her imprint, not erase it.[*]

The principle of not harming, and especially not killing, does not lend itself to degrees. It is not a spectrum. When Sam would fall back on his refrain of moderation, I'd make an analogy to someone who beats his or her spouse. "It's not okay even if you only do it once in a while," I would respond. "You can *never* do it." While the harm from beating a spouse is direct and noticeable and the victim human, the harm in eating meat is just as real and relevant. The pastrami Sam ate was a cow, and that cow suffered and died for that sandwich.

---

[*] As discussed, you can eliminate completely the animal agriculture component of your imprint.

If you share my absolutist view of not harming, then eating meat and dairy is not okay—even a little. A vegan diet allows us to practice complete nonharm. We don't have to hurt *any* animals. Why would we?

Dr. Barnard has an interesting health perspective on moderation, advising against eating any meat or dairy. "Moderation does not apply to things that hurt you."[124] From a moral perspective, I would paraphrase him and say moderation does not apply to things that hurt others.

People who invoke moderation send conflicting messages. In affirming the virtue of restraint, they acknowledge the harm caused by the activity. If it were harmless, moderation would not even be under consideration. At the same time, they justify that harm on the grounds that it could be worse—they are not causing as much harm as they could be. But good acts do not negate bad ones. You are still causing suffering, even if less often.

*

That said, insofar as moderation reduces meat consumption— even if it doesn't eliminate it—it is beneficial and to be encouraged. Mike sees enormous value in the cumulative effect of people cutting back on meat to any degree:

> *If your goal is protecting the well-being of as many animals as possible, you'll have the greatest success by influencing a large number of people to make small changes in their choices. Hitting singles instead of home runs....*
>
> *It's not an all-or-none phenomenon. The more people you can get to make choices, either a little bit or a*

lot — I would say four times out of five when presented with a good option for a meatless food item, I will choose a nonmeat choice. That makes an impact. If everybody did that four out of five times, it would make a pretty big impact. Or even one out of every two times. It would spare many lives. If your book results in forty million people choosing vegetarian or vegan three times more per week, that will help more animals than if the book results in converting a thousand people to veganism.

Complete abstention from meat and animal products — veganism — is the goal, but we go at different speeds and get off at different places. Any step along the path is positive. If moderation in eating meat helps reduce your cognitive dissonance, the animals benefit. Being vegetarian is better than not, and eating less meat and dairy is better than eating more. If everyone ate like Sam and Mike, the world would be a much kinder place.

Sentience

The sickly boy lay in bed until noon every day, nothing but the distant shouts and laughter of his schoolmates playing and his own thoughts to fill his head. And what a head it was. He would become not simply the preeminent philosopher of his day but one of the all-time giants, his influence felt for centuries, persisting even today. His seminal assertion — cogito ergo sum (I think, therefore I am) — is familiar to philosophers and laypeople alike. His mathematical prowess was no less, laying a cornerstone of modern geometry that still bears his name.

René Descartes lived during a pivotal time for Western thought, and for animals. It was the dawning of the Age of

Reason, of which he would become a symbol. It also coincided with the emergence of vivisection, the scientific term for animal experimentation. A cruel practice under any circumstances, it was rendered particularly barbaric by the absence of anesthetics, not yet discovered.

Not only did Descartes fail to condemn this practice, he partook of it, describing one such experiment:

> If you slice off the pointed end of the heart in a live dog, and insert a finger into one of the cavities, you will feel unmistakably that every time the heart gets shorter it presses the finger, and every time it gets longer it stops pressing it. This seems to make it quite certain that the cavities are narrower when there is more pressure on the finger than when there is less.[125]

Descartes defended his actions through a philosophical construct that compares bodies—both human and animal—to automatons, or machines. He believed animals are distinguished from humans by their inability to communicate their thoughts with words or signs, leading him to claim they lack reason or intelligence:

> For it is highly deserving of remark, that there are no men so dull and stupid, not even idiots, as to be incapable of joining together different words, and thereby constructing a declaration by which to make their thoughts understood; and that on the other hand, there is no other animal, however perfect or happily circumstanced, which can do the

> like.... And this proves not only that the brutes
> have less reason than man, but that they have none
> at all.[126]

Descartes concluded that because they lack reason, mind, or thought, animals cannot experience pain. Their howls are nothing more than an instinctual reaction that comes about not "through understanding but solely through the disposition of their organs."

The Cambridge Dictionary defines sentience as "the quality of being able to experience feelings." Sentience includes both physical sensations and emotions and was why, as a thirteen-year-old, I reacted so strongly to my observations of the animal world: its inhabitants felt, and because they felt, they suffered.

It's hard to understand how anyone, let alone someone with Descartes's intellect, could deny animal sentience. The evidence is overwhelming that animals feel pain, communicate with each other, possess intelligence, lead rich emotional lives — are sentient in every sense of the word. It seems self-evident that when a lab animal howls, he is suffering. Charles Darwin observed, "We have seen that the senses and intuitions, the various emotions and faculties, such as love, memory, attention, curiosity, imitation, reason, etc., of which man boasts, may be found in an incipient, or even sometimes in a well-developed condition, in the lower animals."[127] Hume pretty much sums up my thoughts on the subject:

> Next to the ridicule of denying an evident truth, is
> that of taking much pains to defend it; and no truth
> appears to me more evident, than that beasts are
> endow'd with thought and reason as well as men.

> The arguments are in this case so obvious, that they
> never escape the most stupid and ignorant.[128]

Or, as my mother the philosopher used to say, "How can someone so smart be so stupid!"

Denial of sentience plays a straightforward role in reducing cognitive dissonance associated with eating meat. Compassion, the basis of the moral imperative, arises because animals feel pain and suffer. Bastian and Loughnan conclude, "People will, therefore, only experience dissonance to the extent that they consider the target of their action to have the capacity to suffer from harm."[129] In the absence of suffering there is no moral issue. By accepting Descartes's view—which still has its adherents—people sanction literally any treatment of animals, however inhumane.

Anthropomorphism

An animal's similarity to humans plays a pivotal role in how we treat him. Anthropomorphism refers to the attribution of human characteristics to nonhumans. Researchers examining the relationship between anthropomorphism and eating meat note that studies consistently show that anthropomorphizing animals promotes pro-animal attitudes. Seeing similarities between humans and animals increases our perception of their mental capacities. This in turn leads to a reduction in speciesism and increased concern for their welfare. A higher tendency to anthropomorphize animals correlates with greater empathy and less meat consumption. Conversely, dehumanizing animals reduces negative emotions, such as guilt, associated with eating them.[130]

One group of researchers define dehumanization, also called infrahumanization, as the denial of characteristics commonly perceived as uniquely human—such as intelligence, reasoning, and secondary emotions—in the members of an outgroup, either human or animal. Dehumanization is used as a tool or strategy to morally disengage from crimes perpetrated by one's own group. Vegetarians ascribe to animals more characteristics commonly perceived as uniquely human. For meat-eaters, the notion of human uniqueness minimizes the psychological cost of eating animals and creates a "wall of indifference."[131] If animals lack human-like feelings, we are justified in killing them. They conclude, "moral disengagement of meat-eaters might substantially reduce the anthropomorphic perceptions of animals."

As Lex frames it, *"We don't see personality, so it's much easier to kill an insect than to kill a dog."*

*

Anthropomorphism can be manipulated. You may be familiar with The Laughing Cow cheeses, which date back almost a hundred years. Their advertising is a classic example of anthropomorphism employed to reduce cognitive dissonance. Their mascot, which first appeared in 1929, is a cow wearing earrings and displaying a broad smile. Cows, of course, neither laugh nor smile. As we know, the life of a dairy cow is not a happy one. A study of the representations of food animals in consumer culture, titled "The Pig Who Wanted to Be Eaten," examines this strategy:

> "The Laughing Cow," armed with its anthropomorphic ploys, serves to distract consumers from the reality of the animal agriculture industry in

which cows are seen as objects, not humans.... The cows' endorsement also acts as a safety net of reassurance to the consumer: "They are anthropomorphised to ensure that we don't perceive cows as animals, forced to serve humanity's needs all their lives." By humouring the cows' anthropomorphism, the advert also eludes to their reality as the "other," something very separate from man, in fact mastered by man.[132]

Grauerholz describes the use of anthropomorphism by Chick-fil-A:

A more interesting marketing strategy is the use of animals in clearly recognizable forms to sell meat products because such images make use of more complicated and often contradictory messages. The highly successful Chick-fil-A ["Eat More Chikin"] campaign ... is a case in point. By encouraging people to eat chicken, these clever cows (but not too clever for they cannot spell correctly) are transparently self-serving but in the process, they draw attention, if only momentarily, to the fact that some animals are being sacrificed. These anthropomorphized cows have obvious appeal to consumers ... but sympathy does not seem to extend to those chickens being served up at Chick-fil-A restaurants.

On the surface, it also seems illogical that "cute" animals such as the Chick-fil-A cows are so effective at getting humans to eat them or other animals. One might assume, for instance, that the presentation of live or cutely illustrated animals would humanize animals and make their slaughter and consumption more problematic by reducing the emotional distance between humans and non-human animals. Interestingly, the opposite seems to occur. Anthropomorphism and neoteny* increase the emotional distance between humans and non-humans and allow for the exploitation of non-human animals.[133]

*

The title "The Pig Who Wanted to Be Eaten" points to another subtext of the Laughing Cow ads—the suggestion that animals want to serve humans. As Plous observes, "Animals are often described as benefiting from being used, as being content with their lot, as being insensitive to pain, unintelligent, unaware, or wanting to be used."[134] Jonna talks about the cows on a local farm:

> They have four or six cows living up there. These cows, man, they have some of the best views in the freakin' nation. They enjoy a very good climate. They have really good lives, and that's the way I think it should be. They're happy, healthy cows, and all cows should be that way. I don't think that means you couldn't take one of those cows and slaughter them. I think you could. I don't think it's unethical to do that....

---

* Neotony is the retention of juvenile characteristics in adult animals.

> *Taking the life of a cow serves a purpose. It serves the purpose of giving nutrients to a lot of people.*

In *Eating Animals*, Jonathan Safran Foer interviews Bill, a vegetarian cattle rancher unaware of the irony, who shares this perspective:

> *As I see it, animals have entered into an arrangement with humans, an exchange of sorts. When animal husbandry is done as it should be, humans can provide animals a better life than they could hope for in the wild and almost certainly a better death.... I believe it's a noble thing to be raising animals for wholesome food — to provide an animal a life with joy and freedom from suffering. Their lives are taken for a purpose. And I think that's essentially what all of us hope for; a good life and an easy death.*[135]

This creative mixture of anthropomorphism and anthropocentrism functions as an inventive dissonance reduction strategy.

The notion that killing an animal is justified as long as you raise it benevolently conjures up images of H. G. Wells's *The Time Machine*, where the hero is transported to a future world that appears at first to be a Garden of Eden. Ominously, the inhabitants, the human Elois, are all young. We find out why when a siren wails, causing everyone to fall into a trance and start marching in the same direction. It turns out creatures living underground — the Morlocks, descendants of humans — are providing this utopia in exchange for killing and eating the Eloi when they come of age. This picture of humans raised for food is intended to be, and is, horrific. For me, so too is the rearing and killing of animals for food, however well we treat them.

Taboos

Almost all societies have taboos against eating certain animals. A study comparing food taboos across seventy-eight cultures finds that "most societies seem not to exploit the full range of animal products available to them—many animals are 'unconsciously tabooed' in that, while not explicitly proscribed, they are simply not considered food."[136] Taboos vary and include such common food animals as pigs, fishes, and cows. While most Americans would not eat a cat or dog, in some societies they are standard cuisine.

Ori observes, *"We're like, 'Oh, I wouldn't kill a dog. I wouldn't eat a dog. But this animal's okay, or this or this or this.'"* When I asked Eve about the fact that dogs are eaten in other cultures, it was clear she and her family had given it some thought. *"My kids kind of convinced me that there's no difference between eating a dog or a cat and eating a cow."* Eve does put porpoises and elephants in a different class, as we saw in chapter four.

There are various explanations for taboos, but I don't find them particularly helpful in answering the foundational question of why we eat meat. If you're interested in exploring this subject further, I refer you to the study mentioned above.

Normalization

In the next chapter we'll consider the role of societal norms in shaping us and our values. As a dissonance reduction strategy, normalization serves a critical function by quelling any doubts about the morality of eating meat, obviating the need for uncomfortable self-examination—if everyone does it, it must be okay. It also provides moral cover, allowing us to deflect our sense of personal responsibility—I'm just doing what everyone does. But these rationalizations do not change the fact that eating meat has moral consequences, regardless of how others choose to act.

Unlike other reduction strategies, we have no control over normalization. By definition, it's determined by society. We can, however, recognize its invisible hand and the influence it has on our personal choices.

Habit Revisited

Like most people, I have a regular morning routine. I wake up, put my pillow to the side, lie on my back for a few minutes, roll out of bed, get into my sweats, turn on the heat, use the bathroom, drink a glass of water, meditate for an hour, drink another glass of water, prepare breakfast, eat, put my dishes in the sink, fill them with water, check email, read the news, start working. I left out some details, like how I make breakfast the same way every day, but you get the idea.

In addition to playing a critical role in our desire for meat, habits alleviate cognitive dissonance by reducing decision making. Even though we have many choices in the morning, habits effectively eliminate them. We act reflexively, giving little or no thought to our actions. As Neal explains, this is an important adaptation mechanism:

> Contemporary research in psychology shows that it is actually people's unthinking routines — or habits — that form the bedrock of everyday life. Without habits, people would be doomed to plan, consciously guide, and monitor every action, from making that first cup of coffee in the morning to sequencing the finger movements in a Chopin piano concerto.[137]

Dissonance only arises if we actively reflect on our behavior and the harm it might be causing. Bastian and Loughnan explain how this applies to the meat-paradox:

> Reducing the extent of conscious reflection is … a powerful way in which people can guard against dissonance. Habits are especially effective in achieving this aim because they lead to relatively automatic behavior.... Habits can lead to the initiation of behavior without intention and can run to completion without conscious reflection.... By developing habits around meat-eating, people may be able to enact this behavior with little conscious reflection on the consequences, thereby reducing the likelihood that issues related to animal suffering will become salient. Habits literally allow people to engage in meat consumption without

reflection and therefore to avoid the experience of dissonance.[138]

Syl talks about this:

> [T]here's a sense in which there's a normative system that we operate by and that makes us go about it without thinking much about it. And that's a good thing. If you read any history book, they'll say it saves us a lot of mental energy. We don't have to think about "Is it right to do this? Is it right to do that?" We have a system.... We need to create a new system, a new pattern of habits.

Ritual

Animal sacrifice rituals appear throughout human history. These violent, barbaric practices are no longer widely sanctioned, but many of our active traditions mimic them. Thanksgiving, also known as Turkey Day, has all the ingredients. It is universally celebrated with a highly social gathering. The moment when the headless turkey is placed on the dining room table is singular, the crowd rapturously looking on. The task of carving the bird is a high honor, akin to slaying the animal in an actual sacrifice. The traditional presidential pardon of a turkey underscores its ritualistic nature, drawing a nationwide chuckle as that one lucky animal out of tens of millions is spared, sent to a sanctuary to live out the natural course of his life.

Other holidays involve similarly ritualized meat consumption. The Fourth of July is inextricably associated with the aroma of barbecued meat. For many families, Easter wouldn't be the same without the ham. According to the Bible, Jews must sacrifice a lamb at the beginning of the Passover holiday. While that mandate is no longer taken literally, some form of meat is served during the meal to represent the sacrificial lamb.

Rituals are a double-edged sword. Like habits, they can remove critical thinking. When executed reflexively, they preclude inquiry into their purpose or moral implications. Without this reflection, there is no space for cognitive dissonance to arise. Rituals also play a deleterious role by normalizing harmful behavior, like the killing of an animal.

When performed mindfully, rituals can foster awareness of intention and consequences and lead to behavioral change. During our conversation Julie brought up the subject *sua sponte*, emphasizing their positive side:

> There's a story in the Bible that I read at some point in my life where a lamb is slaughtered, and there's a ritual to it and there's a thanking of the Lord for that food. And I think we've gotten away from that. No matter what we eat, we've lost that connection to it. This animal is part of what we're part of, and if we're going to eat it, we need to be thankful that we have it. I don't care if it's a chicken or strawberries. I think we've lost that connection to our food and being thankful for it....
>
> Ritual creates a pause. It creates a moment where you have to consciously decide to do this. You have to consciously be okay with it, and I think that's what we have given up, delegating to others that responsibility.... Not that we can all go back to it, but if we could just educate people about where it comes from, then

> *maybe we'd be much more appreciative of the animal,*
> *the farmer, the process. I think that's what ritual*
> *means—stop and think and be appreciative and thankful*
> *for the food that you're being given, the food that you're*
> *getting, the food that you're making.*

A survey respondent writes, "*Harvesting an animal is an honorable and sacred act that has been forgotten in the modern age. I do believe that harvesting an animal can be a deeply meaningful and spiritual way of eating.*"

*

I certainly appreciate the benefits of mindfulness, but for me the psychological and sociological components of rituals involving meat serve only one purpose—to make *humans* feel better. For the animal, your motivation is of no consequence. The result is the same. Whatever your intention, feelings, or state of mind, she is still being killed.

Avoidance

Once the initial shock of discovering that most of my fellow meditators were not vegetarian wore off, I tried to engage them on the subject. Since the essence of meditation is facing reality head-on, however uncomfortable, I fully expected a robust give-and-take. Much to my surprise—and consternation—my entreaties fell on deaf ears, were a nonstarter. People shut down, refusing to talk about it. The silence was doubly disconcerting because morality is central to the practice, considered the foundation of spiritual growth. Compassion is a cornerstone of that morality, and every meditator is instructed to not harm animals.

Avoidance is an extreme yet classic response to moral dilemmas. "Individuals seem to have a remarkable capacity for avoiding awareness of inconsistencies unless their noses are quite vigorously rubbed in them."[139] It occurs because talking or even thinking about a difficult subject can trigger acute cognitive dissonance. Avoidance is a defense mechanism when the potential for distress is high. People can easily discuss matters that have negligible moral implications or require minimal behavioral change. Meat-eating is the exact opposite. Both the activity and the moral ideal are held dear.

When people shut down, it's because they instinctively understand that confronting the dilemma might lead to an outcome they really don't want. With the meat-paradox, both alternatives are unacceptable. They can keep eating meat and live with the guilt. Or they can give it up and deprive themselves of one of their most cherished pleasures. It's a no-win situation.

During our interview Lex said something that goes to the heart of cognitive dissonance. He doesn't fit into the category of complete avoidance. Happy to be interviewed, he was open and engaging. But when discussing the idea that the food on his plate was an animal, Lex was candid about limits to that engagement. *"I'm not going to spend a lot of time thinking about it. I'll probably stop thinking about it just because it would be uncomfortable."*

My futile attempts to introduce vegetarianism into my meditation community were mirrored by Emily's experience with fellow environmentalists:

I noticed over the years, attending meetings of other groups, that it's pretty common for environmental groups to continue to serve meat at their events. I've always thought that was strange, because these folks would never consider driving to an event in a Hummer. I think the symbolism really matters. I have seen over the years more and more plant-based diets among stewards of the environmental movement and at major events, but there's a disconnect.

People who work for environmental causes like the taste of meat just like other people.... Everyone likes hamburgers, everyone likes steak, everyone likes hot dogs....

When I directed the Sierra Club, we no longer served meat at any of our public events. We attempted to not serve meat at the first annual meeting that I presided over as the new executive director at Charles River Water Association. That did not go over very well.

The shutting down around veganism is reminiscent of people's refusing to confront past trauma. The mere mention of it can trigger such a negative emotional reaction that they avoid the subject at all costs. Of all the strategies employed to reduce the tension around eating meat, avoidance may be the most prevalent. Unfortunately, it is animals who pay the price.

*

Given the strong, incompatible emotions of the meat-paradox—desire and compassion—the cognitive dissonance associated with eating meat can be powerful. We don't want to harm animals, but we do want to eat meat. It's no surprise that the strategies we use to alleviate the tension are so numerous and wide-ranging. It is only by understanding these often subconscious factors that we can make an honest, thoughtful, and heartfelt choice.

Chapter 8:

More Food for Thought

Ori was raised vegetarian. While attending the University of California, Berkeley, where he majored in peace studies, he and his friends Leor and Mark started Vegan Action. He went on to earn his MBA at Stanford and is now a New York Times bestselling author, business consultant, and speaker. He lives with his wife, a lawyer turned book editor, and their dog and cat in San Francisco.

Ori describes his transition to veganism:

> *I grew up vegetarian. When I was a junior in high school, I started dating this woman. She was vegan, but I didn't know much about it. We went to a Taco Bell where we would always go. As we were standing in line, she explained how the dairy industry isn't very different from the meat industry. They go hand in glove. We talked about it. I had some internal resistance because I love cheese. I didn't want to give it up. Then I realized she was right. When it was my turn to order, I said, "Make that with no cheese. A burrito with no cheese." That was the last time I ever ate cheese.*

Ori explains why he remains a vegan:

> *It's a combination. The biggest reason is that I wouldn't feel comfortable with it personally knowing the harm that it causes, the perceived harm that I see—the harm to the environment, the harm to your health, the harm to animals. If I don't need to eat an animal, why would I?*

*

Many factors other than cognitive dissonance influence our decision to eat or abstain from eating meat and animal products.

American Values

Around the turn of the twentieth century, Joe and Anna Rumatsky and Frank and Paula Blavatnick followed in the footsteps of millions of people before them, emigrating to the United States to escape religious persecution—in their case anti-Semitism. They settled in the Bronx just four blocks from each other, and their children—my parents—met and started their own family. Like so many post-war Americans, when they saved enough money, they left the city for the suburbs, landing in a close-knit garden-apartment community in suburban North White Plains. That's when I entered the scene.

In many ways, except for the trauma of my father's death, my childhood was nothing out of the ordinary. I went to public schools. Sports were the center of my life—little league baseball and a continuous stream of pick-up football and basketball games. As a teen, my interests expanded to girls, rock 'n roll, experimenting with alcohol and pot, and doing as little homework as I could get away with. Among my happiest memories are holidays spent on Long Island with my aunts, uncles, and cousins.

Like most people raised in our culture, I was instilled with values unique to the American experience—free speech, freedom of religion, the five ideals of equality, liberty, democracy, rights, and opportunity embodied in the Declaration of Independence. I was young when Congress passed the 1964 Civil Rights Act but remember the original push for the Equal Rights Amendment. As an adult, these values still ring true to me. They shaped and continue to define my political, social, and cultural perspectives.

When it comes to our relationship to animals, society also shapes our attitude. Starting at birth, the lesson is loud and clear— it's okay to eat them and consume their products. At an early age mother's milk is replaced by cow's milk. Unless you were born into a vegetarian or vegan household, meat was probably a mainstay of your childhood diet. In my house the centerpiece of the meal was a steak or piece of chicken, the small side of vegetables almost an afterthought, eaten quickly so I could get to the "good stuff." Advertising for meat is ubiquitous and emotional. Next time you watch TV around dinnertime, notice how many ads are for food, meat in particular. The message is not simply that meat is delicious. It's also sexy and powerful.

The notion that animals are here for our benefit permeates our culture. The existence of zoos and circuses sanctions the practice of taking them from the wild to showcase in cages. Leather not only clothes us but is the material of choice in luxury cars and furniture. Hunting and fishing are widespread, glorified by a large segment of the population. Despite their patent cruelty, rodeos remain legal. Some of this is starting to change. Zoos are moving toward a sanctuary-based model, and Ringling Brothers stopped using elephants before finally closing down. Fur coats, while still worn, are widely stigmatized. These incremental steps are positive but only go so far. They don't fundamentally redefine our relationship to animals. We still do with them pretty much as we please.

Perhaps the single most determinative factor shaping our attitudes and behaviors is the societal norms of the culture in which we are raised. We are profoundly conditioned by the values imprinted on us early on and throughout our childhood. They are ingrained in a deeply visceral way. Because of this conditioning, it's difficult to reject them. They feel right. It's hard for me to imagine not treating women equally or not believing in basic human rights like liberty. Jonna acknowledges the power of our upbringing: *"If I had been raised on a vegan diet, I probably wouldn't even consider eating animals."*

As discussed in chapter four, when it comes to the big moral questions, society often gets it wrong. When it comes to eating animals, we are getting it wrong now. It's extremely difficult to reject a foundational part of our upbringing. But if we are to evolve both as individuals and as a species, that's the task before us.

Avoidance Revisited

In the last chapter I identified avoidance as a cognitive dissonance reduction strategy. People also avoid the subject of eating meat for reasons other than tension reduction. Meat is so commonplace—normalized—that for many, the notion that the routine act of eating presents an ethical issue doesn't occur to them. They are not avoiding the subject to reduce tension. There is no tension.

Society condones meat-eating, so there's nothing to talk or think about. Lex articulates this notion, coming back to it several times:

> *Since we've grown up that way, it's not something we really think about.... Again, I wasn't raised to really think that killing animals is that bad of a deal. I eat them for food.... My morality is probably designed around generally what I've been raised with in society.*

One survey respondent sums it up succinctly when asked why she never became vegetarian or vegan: *"It hasn't crossed my mind."*

Not having considered this issue doesn't mean you don't value morality—you may be the most ethical person in the world. Faced with a morally ambiguous circumstance, you might have a very strong sense of right and wrong. But the moral issue involved in eating meat is not salient or germane for you. In the absence of an obvious or immediate ethical dilemma, there is no cause to consider one.

Failure of the population at large to appreciate the existence of a moral issue is characteristic not just of veganism but of other social movements as well, which is why they are so slow to develop. It's hard to get people to recognize that something is wrong when society says it's okay. If people don't see a problem, there's nothing to engage about, no action to take.

*

Speciesism asserts that humans are more important than other species. Anthropocentrism holds that they are the center of the universe. This belief in human supremacy, common among humans, often entails the complete exclusion of animals from moral consideration. Even when animals are recognized as having inherent value and understood to suffer, this mindset can lead people to underappreciate their suffering. They view it as being of a different kind from human suffering, not as intense, important, or significant.

In some cases this attitude may be explained by lack of exposure to animals, by never having witnessed firsthand their emotionally and intellectually rich lives. You may remember the survey respondent who had a transformative relationship with a pig: *"I originally became [a vegetarian] (believe it or not) when I made friends with a pig. A friend had one as a pet, and I felt guilty."* Sad to say, the effect eventually wore off and he *"woke up one day and craved a burger!"* This explanation has its limitations, since most households in the United States have a dog or cat, animals with highly sensitive natures, yet continue to eat meat.

There are a number of sanctuaries throughout the country, like Animal Place in California, where you can interact one on one with cows, pigs, chickens, turkeys, and other animals people usually meet close up only on their plate. This can be a life-altering event for children, who are predisposed to see animals as individuals rather than food. Places like this are models for the type of transformed world envisioned by veganism.

*

For many people, perhaps most, life is a constant, nonstop struggle. We do our best just to stay afloat and not get overwhelmed by day-to-day challenges. When absorbed with their own problems, people simply don't have the internal space to reach beyond them. From this perspective, delving into the moral issue of eating animals is a luxury most people can't afford. Eve observes:

*Most people are just struggling to get any food to eat,
period. I feel also it's something that people with privilege who can choose their diet can do.... It seems like a
privileged position to be able to choose to be a vegan or
a vegetarian.*

Even when people are concerned with social justice issues, as
Eve is, veganism can slip through the cracks:

*Where I live there are so many other issues that concern
me more. That's where my energy and focus go for the
most part—the carceral state and economic justice and
climate change, although I know veganism is very much
connected with climate.... It's just not something that
occupies my mind space. There's a lot more that I'm
thinking about when I'm eating....*

As difficult as our struggles are, they pale in comparison to
the hardships faced by food animals. It doesn't take much to become vegan—a simple determination. A friend of mine once con-
fided that the amount of suffering in the world was overwhelming for her. Even if she stopped eating meat, it wouldn't make a
difference in the grand scheme of things. I certainly commiserate
with her. The way people treat not only animals but each other
can lead to despair. As I see it, this is not a reason to continue contributing to the problem. It's a reason to stop.

*

Two goals of this book are to stress the urgency of the vegan imperative and to underscore that eating has moral implications,
whether we like it or not. We cannot be passive. When we eat

meat, we actively harm animals. Avoidance does not alter or minimize this fact. If you've read this far, you're not engaging in avoidance, and that's commendable. It takes courage to question your long-held beliefs and behaviors and be open to altering them.

Drawing Lines

Ori used to tell a joke: How many vegans does it take to screw in a lightbulb? A hundred. One to screw in the lightbulb and ninety-nine to check the ingredients. This vegan humor might seem funnier after you've been a vegan for a while. Once you make the commitment, you're likely to spend an inordinate amount of time reading food labels, looking out for things like whey and gelatin. That's one reason Vegan Action introduced the "certified vegan" logo. It's a relief to see it and know you don't have to scan the ingredients.

Regardless of your level of diligence, the notion that no one is morally pure applies to veganism—no one can be a pure vegan. Animal products are ubiquitous, found in such common items as tires, drywall, and paints. Car tires use stearic acid, a product usually derived from animals, although Michelin uses a plant-based version of this ingredient. Car dealer Arnold Clark points out, "When you begin to understand that animal fats are used in the production of steel and rubber among many other components used in car manufacturing, you realise that it is currently almost impossible to buy a car that is 100% vegan friendly."[140] This doesn't mean we don't aim for purity, but it's a reminder that even veganism has its degrees.

It's an inescapable reality that in the course of our lives, just to be alive, we inevitably cause suffering. It's unavoidable. While discussing pure veganism and why she indulges in cow's milk in her latte, Emily, a philosophy major in college, talks about this:

> *In the real world—we do all live in the real world— everyone does the best they can, and of course there's different lines. We probably shouldn't buy clothes that are made by any child laborers, but who looks into that? We shouldn't buy chocolate—there's horrible cruelty in that industry. Diamonds. The mineral industry for iPhones. So all of our behavior and our purchases have a moral component to them. I think your diet is a little weird because you're clearly eating a part of an animal or not, so in that case maybe it should be a little easier.*
>
> *Every single decision we make. Me having three kids—how freaking selfish was that in a planet with way too many people in it?... Just like when I buy an iPhone, just like when I buy chocolate, there's suffering in virtually every decision I make.... We do our best.*

Jonna provides a similar perspective:

> *I don't think there are any easy answers in all this stuff. It's all about trying to find a balance, doing the best you can with what you have. Honestly, I feel like in American society it's often very, very difficult to do the right thing. You go out and buy a gadget or buy a piece of clothing, and it's been manufactured by four-year-olds who are making sixty cents a day. Where is the ethics in that, right? But on the other hand, you have to wear*

something. I definitely think there are a lot of dynamics in society that make it very, very difficult to make truly ethical choices. I wish it wasn't the truth. I think that's the reality we're dealing with.

Lex also takes a practical approach:

We live in a world where a lot of issues upset you.... Do you want to wake up every morning thinking about each and every thing out there that you might have a problem or issue with? That's not a great way of going about your life....

How much do you change your lifestyle to prevent suffering around the world? Literally, you could almost go to the stone-age days and be a caveman living in a cave, grabbing nuts off the ground. At that point you might not create suffering.... I don't think that's human nature. It's like a communistic type of "Hey, we all work for the benefit of everyone else." How deep do you take that morality?

Ori explains what guides him:

I think that we all make choices, and the choices can engender suffering, or not. I go on planes. Are planes bad for animals? Absolutely.... I think you need to look at the harm. How much harm are you doing to animals, environment, health, and do you feel comfortable with it? Make the decision, but make it not based on fanta-syland.

The fact of degrees does not relieve us of moral responsibility. I agree that most actions have moral implications, even if we don't always recognize them. But when it becomes apparent that an ethical issue is involved, we have the power to make the choice that entails the least harm. When it comes to eating, knowing that veganism minimizes suffering, we have the option—I believe the duty—to choose plant-based over animal-derived.

Even though none of us is perfect, we can *aspire* to be. Emily, who agrees veganism is the ideal, explains why she doesn't quite live up to that standard:

> *It's just part of being human. We all have aspirations, and then we do our best. I wish I didn't yell at my children. I wish I was a better boss. I wish I was nicer all the time. I wish I was more thoughtful. So I wish I was vegan. I certainly aspire to be better. Every time I read another article or see another movie and get newly inspired, I get a little closer. But maybe being fifty-one years old, I'm not too harsh on myself.*

We can accept our human imperfection while still striving for betterment. Veganism is no different in this sense from any other aspirational ideal.

*

One of the questions raised by veganism and vegetarianism is where to draw the line in defining animals. Are oysters animals? How about insects? Regan acknowledges the difficulty:

> Line drawing challenges arise for anyone who believes that all animals are subjects-of-a-life.

Amoeba and paramecia, for example, are in the world but not aware of it. Where exactly on the phylogenic scale do subjects-of-a-life appear? I have always believed that no one knows the exact answer, and I personally have never tried to give one.[141]

To minimize disputation, he draws a line at "mentally normal mammals of a year or more" with the understanding "that other sorts of animals might be subjects-of-a-life."

Lex discusses this notion:

> *We're eating something. You could actually argue rais-*
> *ing plants, clearing fields, is killing animals—killing*
> *bugs so that they don't eat the plants. Do bugs have any*
> *more right to live than a dog? Does a dog have any more*
> *right to live than a cow? Does a cow have any more right*
> *to live than a human?*
>
> *So, I think whatever we do to produce something,*
> *there is going to be some death associated with it. Now*
> *you're getting to the point where plants are even talking*
> *to each other, so do plants have a right to exist? How far*
> *down are you going to take the morality of it?*

People will inevitably draw different lines, but the principles of compassion and nonharm remain. From my perspective, any reasonable line includes the animals we eat most often, like cows, chickens, pigs, and fish. They indisputably suffer and have lives deserving of respect.

Suffering and Dying

There's a common phenomenon I admit to not quite understanding. Many people are deeply distressed by animal *suffering* yet unmoved by the thought of *killing* them. Jonna articulates this:

> A lot of my reasoning for becoming vegetarian at the time had to do with the suffering of farm animals. The horrific conditions that factory animals are forced to endure just breaks my heart. Just breaks my heart. Personally, I don't think that eating animals in principle is immoral, but I do think that treating them the way that they're being treated in factory farms is enormously immoral....
>
> I think if you kill them in a humane way so they don't suffer, there's absolutely no problem with that ethically. But I do think they have the right to a happy, healthy life.

Eve shares the sentiment:

> I think that killing them as quick and painlessly as possible is part of the way humans have for a very, very long time gotten their nourishment. Raising animals in a way that causes them a great deal of suffering and also ends up being very unhealthy for the planet and the environment is something that should be changed.... I feel uncomfortable with it. I think it is wrong....
>
> Even if human beings have eaten animals a long time, it's only recently that they've been raised in this

kind of way. It involves a lot of cruelty.... There are cer-
tain types of meat — I would never eat foie gras because
that has always been associated in my mind with suffer-
ing. I never wanted to eat veal because that seems like
an incredibly cruel type of meat to have.

There's something about veal that seems to touch a nerve — it is often singled it out as a meat people avoid. Many people make an effort to eat only organic meat or "free-range" eggs, believing this entails less harm.*

Not causing suffering is important, but morality is more ex-pansive than this. It includes abstaining from killing, which is a monumental harm. When you kill an animal, you take away that which is most precious to all beings, depriving her of the pleas-ures and joys inherent in life itself. The animal no longer suffers, but she has nevertheless been grievously harmed.

While some slaughterers may strive to be humane, there is no such thing as a "painless death." It's impossible to separate kill-ing, an inescapably violent act, from suffering. The animal usually senses the horror in advance, and being killed is a dreadful expe-rience even under the best of circumstances.

Talking about why he tries to not kill insects, Lex touches on this point:

I just don't think I need to kill. As I'm getting older, I
guess I get more sympathetic towards life, just life in
general. I think it's a precious thing. So I understand

---

* As discussed, these labels are misleading. These products involve substantial cruelty.

that we need to kill things to eat, to live, to survive, to defend ourselves, to have our way of life versus some other way of life. But if you don't necessarily have to kill, why? Why do it?

Convenience/Availability/Cost

Sometimes convenience, availability, and/or finances stop people from going vegetarian or vegan. Shelbie, inclined toward vegetarianism in college, describes the obstacles she faced:

> *The thing that stopped me in college was finances—I was a poor average college kid—and convenience. It was inconvenient at that time. All my friends ate meat, or most of them, and they ate out a lot. A lot of the foods that I grew up with have meat in them, so it was cultural.*
>
> *The cheapest thing you can buy is fast food, and the cheapest fast food is a one-dollar cheeseburger. I ate cheeseburgers for the most part.... And whenever someone offered me food, they offered me meat. So my buddies would say, "Hey, yeah, we're having a barbecue," and it's chicken, or "Hey, I made stew," and it's beef stew. I worked at a Steak 'n Shake for almost three years, and we got a discount.... There's almost nothing [vegetarian] to eat. You have cottage cheese or salad or French fries. I never cared for chicken fingers, so I always got a burger. That's what there was.*

Now vegetarian, Shelbie talks about how things have changed:

> It's becoming so much easier. I love White Castle, and
> they came out with their veggie burger, and it's incred-
> ible. It is so much better than any burger of any kind
> I've ever had. I've introduced it to most of my meat-eat-
> ing friends and they all like it. And then they came out
> with the Impossible Burger and I had two choices. And
> in the middle of that, they offered the black bean burger
> for a while, and I had three choices!... So it's becoming
> easier and easier. I think the world is moving that
> way.... The more convenient it becomes, the easier it is
> to stick to something. It's human nature.

An aspiring vegan, she talks about the transition:

> It's not a choice I'm ready for. It's not sustainable yet. I
> removed dairy and cheese from a lot of recipes that I
> make. Vegan Parmesan tastes wonderful. But I have to
> find a way to make it sustainable from a convenience
> point of view. I haven't done that yet. I want to find a
> substitute of some form that is going to work for me....
> It has to be conveniently sustainable. I have to be able
> to maintain it and not fall back on something that's
> familiar.

Several survey respondents refer to convenience.

Nonvegetarians:

- *Too time-consuming to find recipes.*

- *It's exhausting work to find the right meals. [I would become vegetarian if there were] more menu options, more quick recipes.*

- *If restaurants had more vegetarian options, I would consider it.*

- *Way too much trouble. Way too lazy to think of how to get protein in my diet. Not "food aware" enough to care. Plus, I can't imagine life without bacon.... I could be vegetarian if someone cooked for me. But the bacon issue would still be a problem.*

Vegetarians:

- *I would say availability, expense, and convenience are limiting factors to being 100% vegan.*

- *[I would become vegan if there were] better and more widespread alternatives.*

- *[I would become vegan if there were] a decent cheese replacement. More options when eating out.*

*

The documentary *The Invisible Vegan Chapter 4: Stay Woke* explores the challenges to eating healthy, vegan food in many minority communities. Among these are cost and "the matter of access.... A lot of minority neighborhoods don't have health food stores." It identifies the notion of a "food desert," defined as "an area where there is not access to either a grocery store or healthy foods within like a mile or more."[142] This is a human social justice issue as well as a vegan one.

*

As you weigh convenience and cost for yourself, keep in mind that animals in the food industry have no choice. They are forced to endure their suffering. For those of us who can, going vegan is worth the effort, for their sake.

I Like It

We all know the power of desire. In the final analysis, the reason most people continue to eat meat is simple—*they like it*, and because they like it, *they don't want to give it up.* Desire outweighs all the compelling arguments for going vegan, even when people agree with them. It's the beginning and end of the conversation.

This was a constant theme in both the interviews and survey responses. When asked what's stopping her from giving up bacon and fish, Julie replies:

> *I think it's the foodie in me. The foodie still looks at food shows and goes, "Oh, that looks really good," and it's a piece of fish or it's something with a dab of butter or something wrapped in bacon.*

Jonna says:

> *At this point I eat meat, but I eat very little meat. I still eat quite a lot of dairy. I loooove cheese, and stuff like that. I like half-and-half in coffee. Those are just some of the things I have not been able/willing to sacrifice.*

Nonvegetarian respondents to the survey write why they eat meat:

- *I enjoy meat and the ethical and moral concerns have not reached a level whereby I am motivated to give it up.*

- *Just couldn't do it. Love bacon too much.*

- *I enjoy the taste of animal protein.*

- *I love the taste of seafood, steak, and chicken.*

- *Love meat too much!*

- *I really like a good burger!*

- *Like meat too much.*

Vegetarians answer why they are not vegan:

- *I have no good excuse; I'm just unwilling to give up dairy and egg products.*

- *Because I like cheese too much.*

- *Because I like yogurt and cheese.*

A friend of mine told me he tried going vegan for a few weeks but gave it up because he got "bored." He recently told me he had a change of heart and, for health and moral reasons, was committed to veganism, but not long after that he said he was wavering about dairy and eggs. We'll revisit the taste of vegan food and the transition process in chapter ten.

The strategies that people use to reduce psychological tension around eating meat, both conscious and hidden, are only necessary because the desire to eat meat is so strong. If it wasn't, there would be a lot more vegans running around. An interesting phenomenon often occurs when people go vegan. Over time they lose their desire for meat. When that happens, it no longer presents a moral quandary. They don't eat meat because *they don't want to eat meat.*

This question goes to the heart of the book. *Does your desire outweigh the animal suffering?*

Willpower

For some, giving up meat or dairy is just too difficult. They lack the willpower. You may recall the woman who became vegetarian after hitting a deer with her car. She is not going vegan because *"cheese and dairy are too hard to let go."* The addictive nature of meat and dairy can make abstention particularly challenging.

The brevity of this section is not meant to minimize its significance. Lack of willpower may be one of the most common and powerful reasons people continue to eat meat.

Compassion Revisited

The moral tension in the meat-paradox stems from compassion — we don't want to cause suffering. Like any human quality, people possess compassion in differing amounts. A sociopath has none. The compassion of a saint is boundless. The rest of us live somewhere in between.

Without delving too much into the nature versus nurture debate, it is likely compassion has a biological component. Studies have reached this conclusion about empathy, a related quality:

Whilst empathy is clearly shaped by early experience, parenting, and other social factors, different
lines of evidence suggest that empathy is partly biological. Empathy is modestly heritable ... and a
few candidate gene association studies have inves-
tigated the role of various genes in empathy.[143]

There may be a correlation between the hormone oxytocin and
empathy:

Converging evidence suggests that the hypotha-
lamic neuropeptide oxytocin (OXT) facilitates empathy. Genetic approaches have consistently revealed associations between individual variations
in the OXT receptor gene and levels of trait empathy in Caucasian and Chinese populations.[144]

On the nurture side, compassion is certainly influenced by our
upbringing. Importantly, it has the capacity to grow. I've experienced this firsthand through a meditation practice called metta,
which involves visualizing someone and sending him or her
loving-kindness. At first the practice was challenging and uncomfortable. Unlike compassion, metta does not come naturally to me.
But by sticking with it, including a two-week meditation retreat
dedicated exclusively to metta, I've gradually internalized it.
Compassion is similar to loving-kindness in its ability to be cultivated.

In my experience, the visceral reaction to animal suffering
plays a crucial role in someone's willingness to give up meat. How
do you *feel* when faced with animal suffering? Are you deeply distressed, or are you relatively impassive? Your level of compassion

for animals may, in the final analysis, be the determinative factor. The more deeply you are stirred by their suffering, i.e., the greater your compassion, the more likely you are to take steps toward veganism. The less moved you are by their plight, the weaker the impetus to change your eating habits.

I have faith in human compassion. Circumstances may make it difficult to act compassionately, but we *want* to. The capacity to foster compassion affords us the opportunity to strengthen this impulse, to expand compassion's reach further and further until it touches all of our actions in every aspect of our life. Giving up meat is an indispensable part of this process.

Cognitive Dissonance Revisited

In the book's introduction I talked about my friend Mike and posed a question: Faced with overwhelming reasons to change, why do kindhearted people—people like you—continue to eat animals and their products? Festinger proposed that when behavior and beliefs are inconsistent—when cognitive dissonance arises—people try to make them more consistent, and we've explored some of the ways they do this. I've tried to answer the question as best I can, but the puzzle remains incomplete. Even if you're not consumed by the issue of animal mistreatment, you still care. You're reading this book. Eating meat causes you some distress—yet you do it anyway.

In the course of our conversation, Emily may have identified the missing piece. However great the tension of the meat-paradox, there are limits to behavioral change. People will only go so far to relieve the stress. At some point, they are just willing to live with it. As Emily frames it: *"There seems to be in the human condition a lot of comfort with cognitive dissonance."*

Vegan, Naturally

In the forty years I've engaged with people on this subject, one response stands out, articulated countless times in a variety of forms: *Eating meat is natural.* "Natural" is a nebulous term, more often connoting a general feeling than a specific notion. It also conflates several points, which I find useful to break down into three discrete arguments.

One meaning of "Eating meat is natural" is that humans are genetically programmed and biologically constructed to eat meat. Since meat-eating is consistent with our physiology, the thinking goes, it is morally justified. This is factually incomplete and logically flawed. Having the ability to do something does not make it morally right. We are also constructed to eat a plant-based diet. We have the capacity to eat meat, but not the necessity. Since a vegan diet is more biologically sound—healthier—than a meat-based one, under this reasoning veganism, not omnivorism, is morally preferable.

Meat-eating occurred relatively recently in our evolution. As Zaraska explains, while there is evidence of meat-eating as far back as 550 million years ago, when the first primates appeared 65 million years ago following the extinction of dinosaurs, they were vegan, living mostly on fruit. About 15 million years ago our ancestors incorporated seeds and nuts into their diet. Between 3 and 4 million years ago, after our lineage split from chimpanzees and bonobos, we were still not meat-eaters, although our diets had diversified to include insects. Physiologically, our guts still could not handle much meat, an overdose being potentially fatal. It was not until "2.5 million years ago [that] our ancestors had become meat-eaters."[145]

Physiologically, we do not have the bodies of carnivores. Contrary to a common misperception, our pointy canine teeth, which are not particularly big or sharp, do not denote a meat-eating nature. Canines are basic teeth for most mammals, including herbivores. Carnassials, which we lack, are used for meat-eating. We don't have carnivorous jaws or the strong temporalis muscles of carnivorous animals like lions, who can kill with their mouths. We have difficulty eating raw, unprocessed meat and need tools to cut through animal skin to reach the flesh. Our lengthy digestive tracts allow for the digestion of plants and fibers, which require longer processing time. Dr. Barnard sums it up succinctly: "We are basically herbivores who are paying a price for our carnivorous habits."[146]

There's some controversy over the role of meat in brain development. According to some scientists, meat is responsible for the large size of our brains and facilitated our migration out of Africa and subsequent spread to all corners of the globe.[147] One researcher argues that meat supplied early humans with not only all the essential amino acids but also many vitamins, minerals, and other nutrients they required, allowing them to exploit marginal, low-quality plant foods with few nutrients but many calories. These calories, or energy, fueled the expansion of the human brain and permitted human ancestors to increase in body size while remaining active and social.[148] But a recent study suggests it was carbohydrates from vegetable sources like tubers that played the critical role.[149] In either case, for modern humans a herbivorous diet is healthier than one that includes meat.

Perhaps the main takeaway of an evolutionary perspective is the indeterminateness of the label "natural." Rather than static, our diet at any moment in history is the result of a dynamic, on-going process, where what is "natural" is in constant flux. If the history of our diet suggests anything, it is that we are not bound by history. Moving forward, we make our own choices, creating a future untethered by the past. Regardless of any benefits gained by eating meat in the course of our evolution, today a vegan diet is not only sustainable but, as evidence suggests, healthier. Whether or not omnivorism or herbivorism is natural in the evolutionary sense does nothing to inform the moral questions meat-eating raises today.

*

"Eating meat is natural" includes the argument that since animals eat other animals, it's okay for us to do. Vegetarian rancher Bill articulates this reasoning: *"But clearly it's normal and natural for animals to eat other animals, and since we humans are part of nature, it's very normal for humans to be eating animals."*[150] Jonna agrees:

> *Death is something that happens. Just like animals eat animals.... Just like I don't think it's unethical for a tiger to kill an antelope, I don't think it's unethical for humans to eat animals.*

Many animals do *not* eat other animals—they are herbivores. Regardless, we do not look to the behavior of animals to determine our morality. Animals engage in many activities that we would find morally unacceptable if done by humans. Our moral compass is guided by principles like compassion, not the actions of other species. In philosophical terms, the observation that some animals eat others is descriptive. It doesn't address the normative question of whether it's morally right for us humans to eat them.

Julie invokes the notion of the "circle of life":

> One of these days I'm going to die, and I'll be fodder for some tree or have my ashes spread over the ocean to feed the fishes. It's the circle of life on the planet, and I think the first step is to manage it better.

It's true that death is inevitable and our bodies get recycled back into the earth—ashes to ashes. This does not mean we can cause the premature deaths of others, whether human or animal, at our discretion.

*

A third meaning of "Eating meat is natural" is that killing animals and eating their meat is an instinctual part of human nature. As Lex puts it, *"Humans from pretty much the dawn of time have been eating animals. It's just in our nature."* But even if eating meat is natural in this sense—and I'm not saying it is—it does not follow that it is moral. Human history is defined by endless war. Ever since we developed weapons, we used them not just to hunt but also to engage in combat with other tribes. History is replete with oppressive acts—slavery and the subjugation and sexual assault of women, to name just two. Some of humankind's worst tendencies are "natural." This does not make them ethical.

The dark side of our nature is why we institute moral rules. Their purpose is to constrain the basest of our instincts. It is the strength of these impulses that makes acting morally so difficult. If we didn't have these urges, there wouldn't be moral dilemmas.

Rationalization

In my first semester of law school, I learned the most important lesson a trial lawyer needs to know: Judges work backward rather than forward. Instead of following the evidence and legal principles to their logical conclusion, as their task demands, they decide what outcome they prefer, then cherry-pick the facts and, if necessary, disregard or misapply case law to reach that result. This, of course, is not unique to law. It's an aspect of human nature that surfaces in any number of situations.

The moral issue of eating meat is no different. People intent on continuing to eat meat will find a rationale. As Ori observes, *"It's easy to tell stories that there's no harm in what you do."* Bastian and Loughnan describe the phenomenon of shifting criteria:

> Critically, perceptions of others' capacities for mental experience are surprisingly flexible. In the case of animals, our perceptions of their internal world shifts to fit the exclusion criteria for moral concern *de jour*; when moral relevance was based on having a soul, this is what animals lacked, and when it required the capacity to reason, animals' cognitive inferiority became conveniently clear (Descartes). These theories of animals' morally relevant qualities provided a useful justification for

their instrumental treatment within human societies. Perceptions of animals' minds may also shift
situationally, when we use them for our own
needs. When animals are perceived to have a reduced capacity to experience pain, suffering, or
understanding, our concern for their welfare generally decreases and eating them becomes less dissonance arousing.[151]

Rationalizing meat-eating is not a new phenomenon. The
Buddha talked about it 2,500 years ago:

Let a person not give power to the many rationalizations given to justify animal flesh eating. What
logicians say under the influence of their addictive
craving for animal flesh is sophistic, delusional,
and argumentative.[152]

It can be difficult to ascertain whether you are rationalizing or
not, particularly since rationalization often occurs on a subconscious level. That's the challenge. In this book I'm asking you to
evaluate your own meat-eating. This includes considering
whether your reasons are sound, or if you are rationalizing.

Vegetarian, but not Vegan

Many people, including some of my best friends, are vegetarian
for moral reasons but stop short of going vegan. One explanation
for this is their visceral reaction to eating meat. It is one thing to
drink or eat an animal's products and quite another to sink your

teeth into her. While the harm may be comparable, with dairy it is more abstract—milk and cheese *feel* more innocuous than meat. The suffering is not as palpable.

Vegetarians are subject to all the factors discussed in this book, including a tendency to think that being vegetarian is good enough. It's more than most do, so there's no need to go further. As with nonvegetarians, avoidance can be a significant obstacle for vegetarians. They like cheese, or ice cream, or baked goods with eggs. Not wanting to give them up, they don't think too much about it for fear of where it will lead them.

As discussed, any step in the right direction is laudable—and going vegetarian is a huge step. If we were all vegetarians, there would be a lot less suffering. But in today's world, if you want to fully refrain from harming animals, only a commitment to veganism is concordant with that worthy goal.

Chapter 9

Social Animals

Eve is committed to her job as a fundraiser, commuting an hour and forty minutes every day from her home in the New York City suburbs to Manhattan. Food is very important to her. At work she orders in and eats at her desk. At home her husband is the primary chef and does almost all the cooking.

When Eve was in her late twenties, she considered eliminating certain types of meats. She went vegetarian the day after watching a documentary about a Polish woman who worked in a chicken factory farm. When she became pregnant, she didn't feel well and felt she wasn't getting enough nourishment, despite trying various recommendations like eating pistachios and spinach. She started eating meat again and hasn't gone back to vegetarianism, although she limits the amount of meat she eats. Eve is somewhat torn and explains why she doesn't return to vegetarianism:

> *I don't have the bandwidth to cook. I have a really stressful job.... I commute more than three hours a day. My husband is happy to be the cook. I don't think he would be a full-time vegetarian.... I know he would not agree to stop having milk and cheese. So I think until I'm really able to take charge of my eating myself—have a sort of parallel system—it's too hard for me to fight with him about this.*

I'm sure I would be a vegetarian if I wasn't married to him. Whether I would take the next step, it's possible. To become a vegan, you have to learn what to cook and how to nourish yourself properly. For me it just seems like too much to take on. It's easier to go with the flow. My husband cooks, and I put that sadness to the side.

Eve is aware of the suffering involved in the dairy industry:

Most people don't realize that cows are in pens and that they're milked in industrial, stainless-steel machines.... A vegan friend has spoken about how calves are torn from their mothers. I am aware of this, so it's with a heavy heart that I have milk and cheese and eggs, besides eating meat.

Eve acknowledges her cognitive dissonance and voices her aspiration:

Anyone who is able to do the sort of mental somersaults that I'm doing about recognizing the way animals are raised so cruelly and still eat them.... Someday, ideally, I'd like to be a vegetarian and to live in a place near milk that I know is raised in a kind way.

*

When I was in fifth grade, my teacher conducted a rather harsh experiment. A volunteer—my friend Owen—left the room to prepare a group discussion. When he was gone, the rest of us were instructed to interact with him when he got back but then gradually talk with each other to the point of completely ignoring him, however much he tried to engage. As the experiment progressed, you could see Owen get more and more flustered, finally resorting to physically shaking one of his friends to make someone acknowledge him.

This cruel classroom experiment, still etched in my memory fifty years later, was a powerful lesson in the role social bonding plays in human life. We're social animals who derive strength and meaning from our interactions with other humans. It's why peer pressure is so effective. Our relationships are central to our being. As Owen demonstrated, the feeling of isolation, even if temporary, can be traumatic.

We saw how difficult it is to internally question the norms you were raised with because of how ingrained they are. When you do challenge them, you face another set of hurdles—the reaction from your friends, family, and society at large. Depending on the institution you're threatening and your social circles, you can face ridicule, scorn, even physical danger.

Today Martin Luther King, Jr., is considered an icon, the supreme symbol of the civil rights movement. It wasn't always like that. According to one poll, at the time of his death his disapproval rating was nearly 75 percent and the majority of African Americans thought he was irrelevant.[153] It's a tragic fact of history that people of peace like King and Gandhi, from whom King drew inspiration, often pay the ultimate price for challenging the status quo. Suffragettes in this country were imprisoned and beaten just three years before gaining the right to vote.

A more curious phenomenon is when people who do follow the rules are penalized. In law school we studied the case of a lawyer whose client admitted to killing several people. The client told the lawyer where the bodies were buried but instructed him not to disclose the information. Without his client's permission, the lawyer was ethically barred from revealing it—attorney-client privilege is sacrosanct. The victims' families were understandably devastated—and furious—but the lawyer held firm to his principles. As a consequence, he was ostracized by the local community and lost both his practice and his wife.

Vegans, of course, don't face the risk of persecution. I used to encounter the occasional ridicule, but veganism is now so mainstream that even this reaction has all but vanished, at least where I live. But less draconian social consequences can play a role in your decision to take this step.

Family Matters

When I first became vegetarian, my mother was not particularly supportive. "David," she would tell me, "I don't understand why you're a vegetarian." When I went vegan ten years later, she would say, "David, I understand your becoming vegetarian. But I don't understand why you're a vegan." Since I had already moved out of the house, it wasn't an active issue, and much to her credit, when I visited she graciously respected and met my needs. If I had gone vegetarian in high school, I'm not sure how it would have played out.

The most immediate social impact of going vegan is the effect on your relationship with your spouse, partner, or family. Even if you're lucky and they're supportive, it's a logistical challenge. Eating vegan is not as simple as throwing some vegetables together. The menu has to expand, placing an added burden on whoever does the cooking. Your options when eating out are reduced, something your loved ones might not appreciate. When family members don't understand or sympathize, these accommodations can foster resentment.

Eve identified this as the major reason she has not gone back to being vegetarian, where her sympathies clearly lie. Given her job, she doesn't have the time or energy to cook, and she's fortunate her husband is happy to take on the cooking responsibilities. Asking him to cook a separate vegetarian meal for her would put too much strain on the relationship, so she eats what he prepares.

Friends Matter

On the ride home from away tennis matches in college, my team would go to a restaurant, all the more enjoyable because the school picked up the tab. The first choice of everyone but me was a steakhouse, where there was virtually nothing for me to eat, particularly since I don't like salad. (Yes, I know—a vegan who doesn't like salad?!) We ended up compromising, alternating between steak and pizza places. As you can imagine, it didn't promote team comradery.

Since sharing meals is the focal point of so many social occasions, eating vegan can have tangible effects on your social life. Dinner invitations come with the potential awkwardness of having to tell your host about your special needs and could stop altogether because of the inconvenience. You might be left out when friends want to eat at a restaurant with no vegan options. A job that involves a lot of social eating can add another dimension of complication. You can minimize the number of these situations, depending on your circumstances, but sometimes (weddings and holidays come to mind) the issue is unavoidable.

A nonvegetarian survey respondent voices this concern:

> *Food is extremely important to me. I consider it one of life's great pleasures and one of the most basic ways to connect with other people.... I don't have strong enough feelings on the matter to make it worth annoying or inconveniencing people I care about (who cook for me and/or whom I go out to eat with).*

Another person cites her reason for not being vegetarian:

> *Lack of food options in social settings. [I would become vegetarian if there were] more accessible options during social events—at home [I am] primarily vegetarian.*

A vegetarian writes:

> *I would not eat any animal products, except that I sometimes do not have any other alternative (like at work), nor do I want to offend hosts, like my parents, by making their task of feeding me more difficult.*

Dr. Klaper sums up the power of social pressure when discussing why some vegans go back to eating meat: "They just get tired of being the odd person out at the restaurant and at home or cooking two meals for their spouses. So most of it is social."[154]

Fortunately, the number of vegan restaurants has increased dramatically in the past few years, and the quality of the food is quite high. It's becoming standard for nonvegan restaurants to include at least one vegan option. When I travel to places less vegan-friendly than California, I'm constantly surprised that most food vendors are familiar with the term "vegan." The change from even ten years ago, when I had to explain it every time, is striking. In today's world, with the popularization of veganism and a general sensitivity to other dietary needs, like gluten-free, finding a restaurant to meet everyone's needs is much easier than it used to be.

No Judgment

As I mentioned in chapter seven, I have an aversive reaction when I'm around people eating meat. I don't see food. I see an animal and all the attendant suffering. It's not pleasant sharing meals where meat is served, so I try to avoid them. I make the analogy to eating a meal in a home where women are second-class citizens, subjected to physical harm. Such societies still exist today. You can imagine being uncomfortable in that environment to the point of not wanting to be there.

For vegans like me, this creates another level of social challenge. When I eat with someone for the first time, I ask if they're willing to eat vegetarian. If not, I won't enjoy the meal and, unless it's unusually awkward, I'll bow out. This can be misconstrued as controlling and/or judgmental, which isn't my intent. I'm simply avoiding an unpleasant experience.

Judgment is a tricky subject, made more so by semantics. When we deem a person's actions morally wrong, we're making a judgment about the *act*. This is very different from judging the person. I prefer the term "discernment"—we're discerning that the act is wrong. We can do this without making a judgment about the person's character. This goes back to the point in chapter one about hating the act but loving the actor. You can discern that an act is wrong without judging the actor.

Fortunately, most of my nonvegetarian friends are extremely supportive, happy to eat vegetarian and even vegan. I'm very appreciative of that. With those less obliging, I share meals infrequently or not at all. It's especially challenging with old friends I don't see often, who may not know the extent to which this colors my world. Learning to navigate this terrain is an ongoing project.

Emily is cognizant of the perceived judgment in asking people to change their behavior:

> Diet is a very personal and emotional issue for people, and cultural, so it's very easy for people to start feeling judged. It's not just diet. People feel judged if you don't want them to drive a certain type of car. In Newton we're trying to ban new fossil fuel infrastructure, so we're going to get pushback on that. People think we're trying to judge their lifestyle. It can be difficult to get people to change their behavior in order to benefit the environment. It's difficult and charged and emotional anyway, and I think meat and your diet is just part of that, but even more so.

Personality Factors

When I started socializing in vegetarian circles, I couldn't help but notice something. I was surrounded by women. My observation aligns with research confirming a correlation between gender and vegetarianism:

[A] number of researchers have discovered that a greater percent of females report being vegetarian. According to a 1992 Yankelovich study, of the 12.4 million people in the United States who called themselves vegetarian, 68% were female, whereas only 32% were male.... Gender (femaleness) was the single biggest predictor of vegetarianism in a large-scale American database.[155]

Studies have also found that vegetarianism and veganism are associated with certain personality traits and worldviews:

Vegetarians have also been shown to differ from omnivores in a number of attitudinal and demographic variables: for example, compared with omnivores, vegetarians report greater concern for environmental issues, are less likely to endorse social hierarchies, and display greater engagement of empathy-related areas of the brain when viewing scenes of human and animal suffering.[156]

One study examined social dominance orientation ("the degree to which individuals endorse antiegalitarian values and support and perpetuate hierarchical group-based systems of inequality") and found that meat-eaters "placed greater emphasis on social power" and had a more "robust and multi-faceted hierarchical domination concept." Vegetarians and vegans "valued equality, peace, and social justice." Vegetarians also placed greater worth on their emotions, while meat-eaters valued self-control and rationality.[157] This is consistent with other research:

Some meat eaters find their consumption less morally problematic than others. Two political ideologies underlying this individual difference are authoritarianism, the belief that it is acceptable to control and aggress against subordinates, and social dominance orientation (SDO), the endorsement of social hierarchy and inequality.[158]

*

Social considerations are unavoidable. They're part of being human and a legitimate factor in life-altering decisions. In considering going vegan, they are weighed against the plight of the animals—also social beings—who are powerless in their mortal predicament. Whatever the inconvenience and other social consequences, veganism is always the compassionate choice.

Chapter 10:

Making the Transition

Shelbie, a special education teacher from Indiana, remembers the first time she made the connection between meat and an animal, when she was nine:

> I've always loved animals.... When someone identified to me that eating meat was eating an animal, that disturbed me. I didn't like that idea. I think it was my grandmother who told me—it was either chicken or bacon—because I asked her. I had recently been to a petting zoo and she said things like, "Yep, pigs are awesome," and I was, like, shocked. Wait a minute. It took me aback. I like pigs. Dead pig. I remember that moment.

Her family were big meat-eaters, so she couldn't do anything about it at the time, but a seed had been planted. A few years later Shelbie had another memorable experience:

> When I was fourteen or fifteen, I was visiting my maternal grandmother. She made fried chicken. I never had homemade fried chicken. I had KFC. She made it and I thought it was weird. My mother never made chicken with bones in it. Ever. She doesn't care for it. So she gave it to me and I started to eat it, and I looked in it and there was blood in the chicken. She was like, "Oh, it just needs to be cooked a little more," and goes back and cooks it. I

was like, "I'm done. Unh-uh. No meat." After that I re-
ally struggled with eating anything that had bones in it.
Never again.

In college Shelbie was strongly influenced by a professor she admired
who had been vegetarian for over forty years, but she still ate meat because of finances and convenience. As she told us in chapter eight, the
cheapest food was cheeseburgers, all her friends ate meat, and anytime
food was offered it was meat. Meat was part of the culture.

In grad school Shelbie's husband developed health problems and
couldn't figure out the cause. After watching the What the Health documentary, they decided to go vegetarian for thirty days, something Shelbie had done periodically on her own. Nearing the end of their experiment, Shelbie discovered she had a tumor on her small intestine and had
to have emergency surgery to have part of the intestine removed. After
the operation the doctor instructed her to follow a low-fiber diet and recommended staying off meat for an additional sixty days to avoid shocking her system. When the time expired and she decided to try a piece of
steak, she got sick. Since then—three years ago—she has been vegetarian. Her husband continues to eat meat, although less than before.

Shelbie talks about being vegetarian:

I've always been extremely creative, and I've always
been described as weird and different and unique and
loud. The groups that I fit into best tended to consist of
people who were artists, creative people, writers, things
like that, and a lot of those people tended to be vegetar-
ian. I admired it. I felt like it was a choice that is respect-
ful. You're making a good choice for the environment.

You care about something. It's something to stand for.... I liked the people. I liked the culture....

When it comes down to it, there's no big reason. There's a lot of tiny reasons, a lot of things that I care about.... This is just who I am now. This is what I do. I always wanted to be this type of person.... I identify with the community. I have three or four co-workers who are vegetarian, and there's something about it that is a connection to someone else. I noticed that I tend to have personality quirks in common with people who are vegetarian. I get along with them better.

*

A lucky few are raised vegan. For the rest of us it's a transition, and the path is different for everyone. Some go vegan as soon as they learn about it, never to eat meat or an animal product again. It was five years between my awareness of animal suffering and the decision to become vegetarian and another eleven before going vegan. As with any lifestyle change, it's important to do it right, or you risk reverting to old habits without having given it your best shot. In this chapter I offer some practical tips that can smooth the road.

Enjoy

Above all, it's critical that you continue to enjoy eating. The biggest concern for those considering the transition is that a vegan diet is bland and they'll be sacrificing pleasure. It's not, and you won't. The eating experience is processed by our brains and includes flavor, texture, mouthfeel, and temperature. Our brains can be rewired to enjoy new flavors and adjust to different sources of the flavors we enjoy. Flavor is a combination of aroma and taste. Our taste buds sense five basic tastes—sweet, sour, salty, bitter, and umami—all of which are provided by plant foods in enormous variety. A vegan diet is anything but flavorless and may actually enhance the gratification you get from eating.

I remember during my first year in law school, new to Philadelphia, eating at a restaurant in Chinatown that changed my culinary life. I thought I had died and gone to vegan heaven. As I found out, the savory stuffed tofu was filled with seitan, a staple of Chinese food for centuries made from wheat gluten. Today, with the burgeoning awareness of the health, ethical, and environmental benefits, there are more vegan products than ever before to help with the transition, including a multitude of tasty meat substitutes. Burger King's aggressive marketing of the Impossible Burger is a testament to both the quality of these "fake" meats and their mainstream availability.

Tofu, made from soybeans, is probably the most common alternative to meat and a staple of my diet. If not properly prepared, tofu dishes can be bland, but once you get the hang of it, you'll come to appreciate tofu's taste and versatility. Other soy-based options include tempeh, whose taste grows on you, textured vegetable protein (TVP), and soy curls. Additional meat substitutes include seitan and other grain meats, lentils—whose texture mimics the mouthfeel and texture of ground meat—and jackfruit. Jackfruit is a fruit native to India whose flesh naturally "shreds," and it is typically used in dishes rich in sauces, like barbeque, teriyaki, and curry.

Giving up eggs was not difficult for me, but for some it's the hardest part of going vegan. There are plenty of egg replacements to experiment with. For scrambled eggs, omelets, or quiche, you can substitute for the flavor with black salt (kala namak) and nutritional yeast. The texture can be simulated using tofu and chickpea flour. There are also commercial products like powdered "eggs," usually based on algae, tofu, or pea protein. When you bake, you can use soda water, vinegar, and baking soda for leavening and pureed fruits and vegetables or silken tofu to add moisture. For binding, there's flax or chia seed, chickpea flour, aquafaba (bean water), and agar agar.

For both me and Ori, the hardest part of transitioning to veganism was giving up cheese. I missed sinking my teeth into a crisp, juicy New York City pizza, watching the stringy cheese stretch and cling tenaciously to the triangular slice as I slowly pulled it away from my mouth. Letting go of other dairy products was less challenging, although I was a pretty big yogurt eater. Fortunately, there are excellent substitutes for almost everything. Alternative ice cream made from soy, almonds, cashews, or coconut is very satisfying, particularly coconut-based, which I find to be the richest. There are plenty of milk substitutes, including oat milk. I've settled on cashew milk, which I make every morning. It's easy. After soaking one cup of raw cashews overnight, blend with four cups of water in a blender, and you have it. (I skip the soaking part and grind the cashews, then blend with water.) Besides being fresh and vegan, it's also environmentally friendly, since you don't have to buy plastic containers. Cashews can also be used to make cream, cream cheese, and ricotta cheese, and in my opinion cashew milk makes the best vegan yogurt.

I have to say that for me vegan cheeses do not totally hit the mark. The cream cheeses are good, but no one has been able to replicate that stringy quality so vital to cheese's appeal. They just don't seem to melt. But people are working on it, and I think it's just a matter of time. If you're interested in experimenting and making vegan cheese yourself, I recommend the cookbook *Artisan Vegan Cheese*. The author, Miyoko Mishimoto Schinner, has several very high-quality vegan cheeses widely commercially available.

Nutritional yeast (sometimes referred to as "nooch"), a common ingredient in vegan foods, imparts a cheese-like flavor and color. It's made from a single-celled organism, *Saccharomyces cerevisiae*, grown on molasses and then harvested, washed, and dried with heat to kill or "deactivate" it. Because it's inactive, it doesn't froth or grow like baking yeast and so has no leavening ability. It's great in cheese sauces or sprinkled on pizza or popcorn and is a good source of the umami flavor. It comes in flake and powder form, and you can find it in most natural food stores. The brand used by most vegans in the United States is Red Star Vegetarian Support Formula because it's a good source of vitamin B-12 and contains no whey, an animal product used in some other brands. Nutritional yeast is sold in the United Kingdom under the brand name Engevita and in Australia as savory yeast flakes.

Nutritional yeast was an important part of Tim's transition to veganism:

> *I was very proactive about what I was doing. I cooked up a nice big batch of wheat berries for a week so I wasn't cooking every day. I had frozen peas. I bought plenty of tofu. And what really saved me was nutritional yeast,*

because it is a nice substitute for salt and gives things an interesting flavor. For example, I put nutritional yeast on tofu which has been in the microwave for a minute. It can taste a bit like an egg. Eggs are very rich and they don't always agree with me. They always taste great, but they were so rich I couldn't digest them very well. So nutritional yeast is a big deal for me.

Beans can also be an important part of a vegan diet. They're loaded with fiber, so they keep you full and satisfied, and they're also packed with protein—on average, a half cup of beans provides seven grams of protein. A daily intake of beans has been shown to decrease the risk of type 2 diabetes, lower cholesterol, reduce the risk of heart disease, and increase longevity. There are hundreds of varieties of beans (also known as pulses, dals, and legumes) that can be cooked in countless ways, including as ingredients in baked goods and desserts.

Going at Your Own Speed

There are two approaches to transitioning to veganism: sudden and gradual. Tim went from meat-eater to vegan cold tofu, but for many this is too daunting, both psychologically and biologically. We saw Dr. Klaper's discussion of the intense craving that results from being raised on too much meat. It may be easier and more effective for you to make a slow transition. You can devote one day each week to eating vegan or abstain from meat and dairy one meal every day. If you're a big meat-eater, you might start by going vegan one meal a week. As you become more comfortable, you can increase the number of vegan meals. For some people, having and setting specific goals can be helpful.

Shelbie, who prefers a gradual approach, discusses her thirty-day experiment:

> *I do not do any large change at once. Never have.... When I make changes, I always do little things and then I hang on to them so they're stable. I hadn't eaten chicken in years — that didn't matter — so I cut down red meat immediately and then I cut out pork. I just kind of did it little by little so that I could get more comfortable.*
>
> *... I used the steps of behavior change and rewarded myself at the end of the day whenever I didn't have any dairy that day or whenever I had a good day or I behaved appropriately. That's how I started those thirty days. After that it was very easy to keep up....*
>
> *All behavior is purposeful. There's a reason you do something. There's a reward. If the reward is not there, you're not going to change the behavior.... Community plays into that a lot. Being a moral vegetarian is something to be proud of, being able to say I support the environment, I support these things. It feels very real, very rewarding. You can say, "Well, I don't eat meat and therefore I'm lowering the carbon emission on the world." Even if it's just minor, I'm still doing something. That's the reward. It depends entirely on your personality, what works or not.*

Shelbie aspires to be vegan, adding, *"I want to move, and I move very, very slowly."*

Lex also advocates for incrementalism:

> *I have a lot of heartburn when [people] try to change the basic stuff that I've been doing for a long period of time.... You certainly can't change society overnight.*

In the transition away from dairy—which can be addictive, particularly cheese—Dr. Barnard and other vegan experts take a different tack, recommending complete elimination and abstinence, allowing your brain and taste buds to recover from the oversaturation of casomorphins and fat. If you are so inclined, you can indulge in plant-based fats that give you the mouthfeel you're craving—avocados and nut butters, for example. You can also try sharp-tasting foods like arugula when you get a craving, and you can use nutritional yeast any way you used cheese. After a month or two, when your taste buds have adjusted and can more easily accept the difference in flavor, you can start to explore plant-based cheeses.

Psychologically, we can think about it another way. We don't crave animal flesh. We crave the fat, salt, flavor, texture, and familiarity, all of which can be provided by plant foods. With this understanding, we can redirect our thinking from the form of our craving—meat, dairy, eggs—to the source of it—fat, etc. We can also rethink our notion of a traditional meal consisting of a main course of meat with vegetable side dishes. Instead, we can look at a meal as a variety of dishes, none of which is the "main dish."

Eating Healthy

If you're a vegan for ethical or environmental reasons, you might not be particularly interested in the health aspects. But whatever your motivation, an inadequate diet that adversely affects your health is a trap for falling off the vegan wagon. There's plenty of vegan junk food out there, like my favorite, tortilla chips. I highly recommend that you keep it to a minimum, particularly at first.

Fortunately, virtually any *well-rounded* vegan diet will be nutritionally adequate. If you like to cook, there are a ton of vegan cookbooks and an endless supply of vegan recipes online. Preparing tasty vegan meals is also a good way to bring disapproving family members around — if not to becoming vegan, at least to not giving you a hard time about it!

If you're concerned about eating well, you could consult a nutrition coach with expertise in vegan food. In this chapter I relied heavily on lectures by nutrition consultant Sherry Morgado, a former diet mentor for Dharma Voices for Animals.[159] The listing Plant-Based Doctors and organizations like the Physicians Committee for Responsible Medicine can also point you in the right direction.[160] In general, the web can be an excellent source of moral and logistical support and for many people makes the difference in sticking with the commitment.

Human Liberation

At thirteen, despite my jarring and profound realization of the univer-
sality of suffering, I did not become vegetarian. Observing that insects
avoided death and seemed to suffer, my first action was to stop killing
them. It wasn't really a decision. It came naturally. I no longer wanted
to kill them. So I didn't.

As you might imagine, this behavior is not always met with understanding. Not long after my father's death, I went on a summer vacation with one of my best friends and his family. To my friend's consternation and annoyance, every time he started to swat an insect—often, as we were in the middle of nature—I intervened. Only thirteen, he did not appreciate the emotional trauma I was carrying from the recent tragedy. Our relationship was permanently strained.

Reaction to my expansive pacifism isn't always negative. Before the first class on my first day of law school, I was talking to a classmate when a cockroach scampered in front of him. Just as he was readying to unceremoniously stomp it with his shoe, I interceded, asking him not to. A discussion ensued, the cockroach survived, and thirty years later we remain friends. We learned something about each other that day, and it cemented our relationship.

I thought about including this subject in the first chapter, since it was a significant stage in my moral development. The reaction I've received over the years gave me pause, leading me to save it for here, at the end of the book. Simply put, a lot of people think it's weird. I decided not to risk alienating those who might otherwise be receptive to the vegan message. I have to say, though, I was heartened after talking to Lex, the former fighter pilot, and finding out he too values insects' lives and does his best not to harm them. Perhaps it's more common than I know.

Insects are encompassed by the Buddhist precept of not killing, which applies to all living beings. During my stay at the Myanmar monastery, I practically lived at the infirmary—digestive problems, acid reflux, rashes, and allergic reactions, to name a few of my maladies. One day, a monk came in to have some ticks removed that had embedded themselves in his skin. After they were carefully plucked, I was about to speak up when I remembered where I was. The monks had no intention of flushing them down the toilet. I watched with a feeling of comradery as they marched into the woods to release them. At a Sri Lankan monastery, I was walking in the woods when I saw an object in the distance lying across the path. This was unusual, since the monks were meticulous about sweeping the paths and keeping them clear. As I got closer, I realized it was a stick placed to protect an army of ants crossing the path that might otherwise have been inadvertently trampled.

I haven't canvassed other vegans about this. It doesn't generally arise, since veganism is primarily about what you eat and what you wear. I think of it more as a spiritual practice than a vegan one, although I see the two as conjoined, both grounded in the unifying principle of nonviolence (*ahimsa*). This ethic is fundamentally transformative, an attitude that benefits not only yourself but also a world in desperate need of kindness and caring.

Most people think of going vegetarian or vegan as losing something, sacrificing an important part of your life. I felt that way when I first went vegetarian. Over time the feeling metamorphosed. Even though I was a big meat-eater up until the very moment I became vegetarian, I gradually lost my desire for it. Today my craving is completely eradicated. The initial feeling of loss has been replaced by a different emotion—*liberation*. It's as though a weight has been lifted. Knowing I'm not harming an animal when I eat has a clean, pure feel to it. It's the lightness associated with the absence of guilt. Doing harm is a burden. Not harming is freedom.

Veganism is an integral component of my spiritual growth. The traditions that inform my path call for the development of the same spiritual qualities—compassion, loving-kindness, and empathy. When these and other qualities are sufficiently developed, we reach a place of deep inner peace characterized by nongreed, nonharm, and nonattachment. When perfected, we attain a state entirely free from suffering. Seen in this light, veganism is not just about animal liberation. It is an essential part of the journey to human liberation.

Notes

Chapter 1: The Moral Imperative

1. Compassion in World Farming, *Strategic Plan 2013–2017: For Kinder, Fairing Farming Worldwide*, p. 5.

2. Food and Agriculture Organization of the United Nations, *Guidelines for Slaughtering, Meat Cutting and Further Processing* (1991), www.fao.org/3/t0279e/T0279E05.htm.

3. L. Marino and C. Colvin, "Thinking Pigs: A Comparative Review of Cognition, Emotion, and Personality in *Sus domesticus*," *International Journal of Comparative Psychology* 28, no. 1 (2015).

4. Patti Breitman, lecture for online course *"The Teachings of the Buddha on Animals,"* 2018.

5. Will Tuttle, lecture for online course *"The Teachings of the Buddha on Animals,"* 2018.

6. Mohandas Gandhi, Autobiography: *The Story of My Experiments with Truth* (Public Affairs Press, 1948), chapter 30.

7. Peter Singer, *Animal Liberation* (HarperCollins, 1975), pp. 5 and 7, quoting utilitarian Henry Sidgwick (italics in original).

8. Tom Regan, *The Case for Animal Rights* (University of California Press, 1983).

9. Josephine Donovan and Carol J. Adams, eds., *The Feminist Care Tradition in Animal Ethics* (Columbia University Press, 2007), introduction, pp. 2–3.

10. Sue Donaldson and Will Kymlicka, *Zoopolis: A Politic Theory of Animal Rights* (Oxford University Press, 2013).

11. Matthew Scully, *Dominion: The Power of Man, the Suffering of Animals, and the Call to Mercy* (St. Martin's Griffin, 2003).

12. Tristram Stuart, *The Bloodless Revolution: A Cultural History of Vegetarianism from 1600 to Modern Times* (W.W. Norton, 2006), pp. 61–62.

13. *Mahaparinirvana Sutra.*

14. www.dharmavoicesforanimals.org.

15. "Animals and the Buddha." *YouTube,* uploaded by Dharma Voices for Animals, October 17, 2014, www.youtube.com/watch?v=S0MWAAykFuc.g

16. *Mother Sutra.*

Chapter 2: The Environmental Imperative

17. Andersen, Kip, and Keegan Kuhn. *Cowspiracy: The Sustainability Secret.* 2014. www.cowspiracy.com/facts.

18. Screen Actors Guild Awards, *"26th Annual Screen Actors Guild Awards Plant-Based Menu"* (press release), January 15, 2020.

19. Chauncey Alcorn, *"Vegan Sneakers Set to Be Next Sustainable Plant-Based Craze in 2020,"* CNN Business, December 16, 2019, www.cnn.com/2019/12/14/business/plant-shoe-vegan/index.html.

20. Testimony of Dr. James Hansen before the U.S. Senate Committee on Energy and Natural Resources, June 23, 1988.

21. Intergovernmental Panel on Climate Change, *"Principles Governing IPCC Work,"* approved October 1, 1998.

22. R. K. Pachauri et al., *Climate Change 2014: Synthesis Report. Contribution of Working Groups I, II and III to the Fifth Assessment Report of the Intergovernmental Panel on Climate Change* (IPCC, 2014), SPM 1, 1.1, and 1.2.

23. U.S. National Climate Assessment, U.S. Global Change Research Program, *Overview: Climate Change Impacts in the United States* (2014), p. 16, www.globalchange.gov/browse/

reports/overview-climate-change-impacts-united-states-third-national-climate-assessment.

24. NOAA National Centers for Environmental Information, *State of the Climate: Global Climate Report—Annual 2020*, www.ncdc.noaa.gov/sotc/global/202013.

25. U.S. Department of Defense, National Security *Implications of Climate-Related Risks and a Changing Climate*, submitted to Congress July 23, 2015.

26. Paris Agreement, article 2, section 1(A).

27. Food and Agricultural Organization of the United Nations, *Tackling Climate Change Through Livestock: A Global Assessment of Emissions and Mitigation Opportunities* (2013), pp. xii and 20; Livestock, Environment and Development (LEAD) Initiative, *Livestock's Long Shadow: Environmental Issues and Options* (2006), pp. 112–14.

28. Food and Agricultural Organization of the United Nations, *Tackling Climate Change Through Livestock*, p. ix; Livestock, Environment and Development (LEAD) Initiative, *Livestock's Long Shadow*, p. xxi.

29. Peter Scarborough et al., "Dietary Greenhouse Gas Emissions of Meat-Eaters, Fish-Eaters, Vegetarians and Vegans in the UK," *Climatic Change* 125 (2014): 186.

30. Stuart, *The Bloodless Revolution*, pp. 401–3. All the quotes in this paragraph are from the same source.

31. Ibid., p. 403.

32. Robert W. Bray, "History of Meat Science," *The 50th Anniversary History of the Reciprocal Meat Conference* (1997), www.meatscience.org/about-amsa/history-mission/history-of-meat-science.

33. Livestock, Environment and Development (LEAD) Initiative, Livestock's Long Shadow, p. xxi; see also Food and

Agriculture Organization of the United Nations, "Animal Production," www.fao.org/animal-production/en/, which estimates that animal agriculture uses almost 80 percent of the world's agricultural land.

34. www.cowspiracy.com/facts, citing John Robbins, *Diet for a New America* (StillPoint, 1987), p. 352.

35. Stuart, *The Bloodless Revolution*, p. 404.

36. Richard Openlander, "Animal Agriculture, Hunger, and How to Feed a Growing Global Population: Part One of Two," Forks Over Knives, August 20, 2013, www.forksoverknives.com/wellness/animal-agriculture-hunger-and-how-to-feed-a-growing-global-population-part-one-of-two.

37. Livestock, Environment and Development (LEAD) Initiative, Livestock's Long Shadow, p. xxi.

38. Union of Concerned Scientists, "What's Driving Deforestation?" February 8, 2016, www.ucsusa.org/resources/whats-driving-deforestation.

39. Intergovernmental Science-Policy Platform on Biodiversity and Ecosystem Services (IPBES), The Global Assessment Report on Biodiversity and Ecosystem Services: Summary for Policymakers (2019), pp. 11–12 (reference omitted).

40. United Nations Educational, Scientific and Cultural Organization, Executive Summary: The United Nations World Water Development Report 2019—Leaving No One Behind, p. 2.

41. Ibid.; www.cowspiracy.com/facts; Pew Commission on Industrial Farm Animal Production, Putting Meat on the Table; Industrial Farm Animal Production in America (2008), p. 27; David Pimente et al., "Water Resources: Agricultural and Environmental Issues," Bioscience 54, no. 10 (October 2004): 911, table 2.

42. U.S. General Accounting Office, Animal Agriculture: Waste Management Practices (1999), pp. 3–4.

43. Livestock, Environment and Development (LEAD) Initiative, *Livestock's Long Shadow*, p. 167; see also Pew Commission on Industrial Farm Animal Production, *Putting Meat on the Table*, p. 25.

44. Livestock, Environment and Development (LEAD) Initiative, *Livestock's Long Shadow*, p. 83.

45. Pew Commission on Industrial Farm Animal Production, *Putting Meat on the Table*, p. 25.

46. National Oceanic and Atmospheric Administration, "Large 'Dead Zone' Measured in Gulf of Mexico," August 1, 2019.

47. Ibid., p. 23.

48. Ibid.; Livestock, Environment and Development (LEAD) Initiative, *Livestock's Long Shadow*, p. 69 (boldface in original).

49. www.cowspiracy.com/facts.

Chapter 3: The Health Imperative

50. Emily Seigel, "Novak Djokovic Opens Vegan Restaurant, Eqvita, in Monte Carlo," *Forbeslife*, August 30, 2016.

51. "Carl Lewis on his Vegan Diet." *YouTube*, uploaded by Kinder World, May 31, 2015, www.youtube.com/watch?v =zBcyUqspQjk.

52. Psihoyos, Louie. *The Game Changers*. 2018.

53. Thomas Campbell and T. Colin Campbell, *The China Study: Startling Implications for Diet, Weight Loss and Long-Term Health* (BenBella Books, 2006).

54. International Agency for Research on Cancer, World Health Organization, *Red Meat and Processed Meat*, IARC

Monographs on the Evaluation of Carcinogenic Risks to Humans, vol. 114 (2018), pp. 488–92.

55. Yessenia Tantamango-Bartley et al., "Vegetarian Diets and the Incidence of Cancer in a Low-Risk Population," *Cancer Epidemiology, Biomarkers, and Prevention* 22, no. 2 (February 2013): 286–94.

56. Yessenia Tantamango-Bartley et al., "Are Strict Vegetarians Protected Against Prostate Cancer?" *American Journal of Clinical Nutrition* 103, no. 1 (January 2016): 153–60.

57. Michael Orlich et al., "Vegetarian Dietary Patterns and the Risk of Colorectal Cancers," *JAMA Internal Medicine* 175, no. 5 (May 2015): 767–76.

58. S. Tonstad et al., "Vegetarian Diets and Incidence of Diabetes in the Adventist Health Study-2," *Nutrition, Metabolism and Cardiovascular Diseases* 23, no. 4 (April 2013): 292–99.

59. Y. T. Szeto et al., "Effects of a Long-Term Vegetarian Diet on Biomarkers of Antioxidant Status and Cardiovascular Disease Risk," *Nutrition* 20, no. 10 (2004): 863–66.

60. Michael Orlich and Gary Fraser, "Vegetarian Diets in the Adventist Health Study 2: A Review of Initial Published Findings," *American Journal of Clinical Nutrition* 100, no. S1 (2014): 357S.

61. U.S. Department of Health and Human Services and U.S. Department of Agriculture, 2015–2020 *Dietary Guidelines for Americans,* 8th ed. (2015), appendix 7, table A7-1.

62. "When Vegan Diets Don't Work #1: Dr. Klaper." *YouTube,* uploaded by Plant Based News, January 31, 2019, www.youtube.com/watch?reload=9&v=u8YlCOCEUsk&feature=emb_logo.

63. "Dr. Neal Barnard: The Cheese Trap – Break the Addiction." *YouTube,* uploaded by Compassionate Living Events, May 11, 2017, www.youtube.com/watch?v=PHyLV3jeifk.

Chapter 4: Speciesism

64. Aph Ko and Syl Ko, *Aphro-ism: Essays on Pop Culture, Feminism and Black Veganism from Two Sisters*, (Lantern Publishing and Media, 2017).

65. Singer, *Animal Liberation*, p. 6.

66. Marjorie Spiegel, *The Dreaded Comparison: Human and Animal Slavery* (Mirror Books, 1996), p. 7.

67. Ibid., p. 28.

68. Ibid., p. 9.

69. Ibid., pp. 15–16 and 30.

70 Scott Plous, *Understanding Prejudice and Discrimination* (McGraw-Hill, 2003), p. 510.

71. Spiegel, *The Dreaded Comparison*, p. 13.

72. Plous, *Understanding Prejudice and Discrimination*, p. 510 (citation omitted).

73. Spiegel, *The Dreaded Comparison*, pp. 27–28.

74. Ibid., p. 30.

75. Ibid., p. 13.

76. Ibid., p. 20.

77. Singer, *Animal Liberation*, p. 20.

78. Regan, *The Case for Animal Rights*, preface to 2004 edition, p. xxiii.

79. Charles Darwin, *The Descent of Man* (J. Murray, 1871), pp. 35 and 10.

80. Susana Monso et al., "Animal Morality: What It Means and Why It Matters," Journal of Ethics, September 27, 2018.

81. Jeremy Bentham, *An Introduction to the Principals of Morals and Legislation* (1789), chapter 17.

82. Spiegel, *The Dreaded Comparison*, pp. 22–23.

83. "Richard Dawkins: 'I would like everybody to be a vegetarian.'" *YouTube*, uploaded by Paul Shapiro, September 29, 2013, www.youtube.com/watch?v=znMBG5DQn14.

Chapter 6: Cognitive Dissonance

84. Leon Festinger, "Cognitive Dissonance," *Scientific American* 207, no. 4 (1962): 93–102.

85. Brock Bastian and Steve Loughnan, "Resolving the Meat-Paradox: A Motivational Account of Morally Troublesome Behavior and Its Maintenance," *Personality and Social Psychology Review* 21, no. 3 (August 2017): 278. See also Steve Loughnan, Nick Haslam, and Brock Bastian, "The Role of Meat Consumption in the Denial of Moral Status and Mind to Meat Animals," *Appetite* 55, no. 1 (2010): 156–59; Steve Loughnan, Brock Bastian, and Nick Haslam, "The Psychology of Eating Animals," *Current Directions in Psychological Science* 23, no. 2 (April 2014): 104–8.

86. Bastian and Loughnan, "Resolving the Meat-Paradox," p. 279.

87. Ibid., p. 3.

88. Melanie Joy, *Why We Love Dogs, Eat Pigs, and Wear Cows: An Introduction to Carnism* (Conari Press, 2010), pp. 17, 26.

89. Marta Zaraska, *Meathooked: The History and Science of our 2.5-Million-Year Obsession with Meat* (Basic Books, 2016), pp. 24 and 28.

90. Hank Rothgerber, "Real Men Don't Eat (Vegetable) Quiche: Masculinity and the Justification of Meat Consumption," *Psychology of Men & Masculinity* 14, no. 4 (2012): p. 364 (citations omitted).

91. M. W. Allen et al., "Values and Beliefs of Vegetarians and Omnivores," *Journal of Social Psychology* 140, no. 4 (2000): 407 (citations omitted).

92. See, e.g., Matthew Ruby and Steven Heine, "Meat, Morals, and Masculinity," *Appetite* 56 (2010): 447–50.

93. David Hume, *A Treatise of Human Nature* (1739; Oxford University Press, 1978).

94. Carol Ann Norton, "Psychological Consistency, Inconsistency and Cognitive Dissonance in the Relationship Between Eating Meat and Evaluating Animals" (PhD thesis, Institute of Social Psychology, London School of Economics and Political Science, 2009), p. 153.

95. David Neal, "Habits—A Repeat Performance," *Current Directions in Psychological Science* 15, no. 4 (2016): 201–2.

96. Bastian and Loughnan, "Resolving the Meat-Paradox," p. 279.

97. L. E. Mayfield et al., "Consumption of Welfare-Friendly Food Products in Great Britain, Italy and Sweden, and How It May Be Influenced by Consumer Attitudes To, and Behaviour Towards, Animal Welfare Attributes," *International Journal of Sociology of Food and Agriculture* 15, no. 3 (2007): 63.

98. Sam Hardy and Gustavo Carlo, "Moral Identity: What Is It, How Does It Develop, and Is It Linked to Moral Action?" *Child Development Perspectives* 5, no. 3 (2011): 212.

99. Ibid., p. 215 (citations omitted).

100. W. Damon and D. Hart, "Self-Understanding and Its Role in Social and Moral Development," in *Developmental Psychology: An Advanced Textbook,* 3rd ed., ed. M. Bornstein and M. E. Lamb (Erlbaum, 1992), pp. 421–64.

101. Martha Stout, *The Sociopath Next Door* (Harmony, 2006).

Chapter 7: Reducing the Tension

102. Norton, "Psychological Consistency," p. 25.

103. Albert Bandura, "Selective Moral Disengagement in the Exercise of Moral Agency," *Journal of Moral Education* 31, no. 2 (2002): 104.

104. Plous, *Understanding Prejudice and Discrimination*, p. 513.

105. 2019–2020 American Pet Products Association National Pet Owners Survey, www.americanpetproducts.org/pubs_survey.asp.

106. Boyka Bratanova et al., "The Effect of Categorization as Food on the Perceived Moral Standing of Animals," *Appetite* 57 (2011): 194–96 (citations omitted).

107. Nora Benningstad and Jonas Kunst, "Dissociating Meat from Its Animal Origins: A Systematic Literature Review," *Appetite* 147 (2020): 104554.

108. Liz Grauerholz, "Cute Enough to Eat: The Transformation of Animals into Meat for Human Consumption in Commercialized Image," *Humanity & Society* 31, no. 4 (November 2007): 339 (citation omitted).

109. Shane Sayers, "'The Pig Who Wanted to Be Eaten': A Discussion on the Representation of Animals in Consumer Culture," *Animal People Forum*, November 24, 2017, www.animalpeopleforum.org/2017/11/24/pig-wanted-eaten-discussion-representation-animals-consumer-culture/.

110. Jonas Kunst and Sigrid Hohle, "Meat Eaters by Dissociation: How We Present, Prepare and Talk About Meat Increases Willingness to Eat Meat by Reducing Empathy and Disgust," *Appetite* 105 (2016): 770.

111. Grauerholz, "Cute Enough to Eat," pp. 347–48.

112. Norton, "Psychological Consistency," p. 22.

113. Megan Earle et al., "Eating with Our Eyes (Closed:): Effects of Visually Associating Animals with Meat on Anti-vegan/vegetarian Attitudes and Meat Consumption Willingness," *Group Processes & Intergroup Relations* 22, no. 6 (2019): 830–31.

114. Grauerholz, "Cute Enough to Eat," pp. 348–49.

115. Mimi Sheraton, "John Updike Ruminates on Matters Gustatory," *New York Times*, December 15, 1982.

116. Bandura, "Selective Moral Disengagement," p. 108.

117. Bastian and Loughnan, "Resolving the Meat-Paradox," p. 286.

118. Norton, "Psychological Consistency," p. 54 (citation omitted).

119. www.youtube.com/watch?v=S0MWAAykFuc.

120. "Official 'Glass Walls' Video by Paul McCartney." YouTube, uploaded by PETA, April 12, 2013, www.youtube.com/watch?v=ql8xkSYvwJs.

121. www.dltk-teach.com/rhymes/macdonald/mlyrics.htm.

122. Adapted from Loren Eiseley, "The Star Thrower," in *The Unexpected Universe* (Harcourt, Brace and World, 1969).

123. Les Mitchell, "Moral Disengagement and Support for Non-human Animal Farming," *Society & Animals* 19 (2011): 51–52 (italics in original).

124. "Dr. Neal Barnard: Are Humans Designed to Eat Meat?" *Facebook*, uploaded by LIVEKINDLY, September 21, 2017, www.facebook.com/watch/?v=608156542866257.

125. René Descartes, *Description of the Human Body* (1647).

126. René Descartes, *Discourse on Method* (1936), part 5.

127. Darwin, *The Descent of Man*, p. 105.

128. Hume, *A Treatise of Human Nature*, p. 176.

129. Bastian and Loughnan, "Resolving the Meat-Paradox," p. 281.

130. Feiyang Wang and Frederic Basso, "'Animals Are Friends, Not Food': Anthropomorphism Leads to Less Favorable Attitudes Toward Meat Consumption by Inducing Feelings of Anticipatory Guilt," *Appetite* 138 (2019).

131. Michal Bilewicz et al., "The Humanity of What We Eat: Conceptions of Human Uniqueness Among Vegetarians and Omnivores," *European Journal of Social Psychology* 41 (2011): 201–202 and 207–208 (citations omitted).

132. Sayers, "'The Pig Who Wanted to be Eaten,'" pp. 8–9 (citations omitted).

133. Grauerholz, "Cute Enough to Eat," p. 348 (citation omitted).

134. Plous, *Understanding Prejudice and Discrimination*, p. 510.

135. Jonathan Safran Foer, *Eating Animals* (Penguin, 2010), p. 207.

136. Daniel Fessler et al., "Meat Is Good to Taboo: Dietary Proscriptions as a Product of the Interaction of Psychological Mechanisms and Social Processes," *Journal of Cognition and Culture* 3, no. 1 (2003): 6 (citations omitted).

137. Neal, "Habits," p. 198.

138. Bastian and Loughnan, "Resolving the Meat-Paradox," p. 284 (citations omitted).

139. Ian McGregor et al., "'Remembering' Dissonance: Simultaneous Accessibility of Inconsistent Cognitive Elements Moderates Epistemic Discomfort," in *Cognitive Dissonance: Progress on a Pivotal Theory in Social Psychology*, ed. E. Harmon-Jones and J. Mills, Science Conference Series (American Psychological Association, 1999), p. 331.

Chapter 8: More Food for Thought

140. Arnold Clark, "Can You Own a Car and Be a Vegan?" May 19, 2015, www.arnoldclark.com/newsroom/780-can-you-own-a-car-and-be-a-vegan.

141. Regan, *The Case for Animal Rights*, preface to 2004 edition, p. xvi.

142. "The Invisible Vegan Chapter 4: Stay Woke." *YouTube*, uploaded by The Invisible Vegan, February 11, 2019, www.youtube.com/watch?v=OibkuM8rh2Y.

143. Varun Warrier et al., "Genome-wide Analyses of Self-reported Empathy: Correlations with Autism, Schizophrenia, and Anorexia Nervosa," *Translational Psychiatry* 8, no. 35 (2018) (citations omitted).

144. Yayuan Geng et al., "Oxytocin Enhancement of Emotional Empathy: Generalization Across Cultures and Effects on Amygdala Activity," *Frontiers in Neuroscience* 12, no. 512 (2018) (citations omitted).

145. Zaraska, *Meathooked*, p. 15.

146. www.facebook.com/watch/?v=608156542866257.

147. Zaraska, *Meathooked*, pp. 29–33.

148. Katharine Milton, "A Hypothesis to Explain the Role of Meat-Eating in Human Evolution," *Evolutionary Anthropology Issues News and Reviews* 8, no. 1 (1999): 11–21.

149. Karen Hardy et al., "The Importance of Dietary Carbohydrate in Human Evolution," *Quarterly Review of Biology* 90, no. 3 (2015): 251–68.

150. Foer, *Eating Animals*, p. 207.

151. Bastian and Loughnan, "Resolving the Meat-Paradox," p. 282 (citations omitted).

152. Mahaparinirvana Sutra.

Chapter 9: Social Animals

153. Tavis Smiley, "The One Single Thing Donald Trump and Martin Luther King, Jr. Have in Common," *Time*, December 1, 2017, www.time.com/5042070/donald-trump-martin-luther-king-mlk; James Cobb, "When Martin Luther King Jr. Was Killed, He Was Less Popular Than Donald Trump Is Today," *USA Today*, April 4, 2018, www.usatoday.com/story/opinion/2018/04/04/martin-luther-king-jr-50-years-assassination-donald-trump-disapproval-column/482242002.

154. www.youtube.com/watch?reload=9&v=u8YlCOCEUsk&feature=emb_logo.

155. Rothgerber, "Real Men Don't Eat (Vegetable) Quiche," p. 364.

156. Ruby and Heine, "Meat, Morals, and Masculinity," p. 447.

157. Allen et al., "Values and Beliefs of Vegetarians and Omnivores," pp. 408 and 417–19 (citations omitted).

158. Loughnan, Bastian, and Haslam, "The Psychology of Eating Animals," p. 105 (citations omitted).

Chapter 10: Making the Transition

159. Sherry Morgado, lectures for online course *"The Teachings of the Buddha on Animals,"* 2018.

160. www.plantbaseddoctors.org; www.pcrm.org.

Acknowledgments

Thanks to: Nancy Brockington, my harshest critic and fiercest defender; Bernard Unti, my vegan brother-in-arms; Peter Fleischer, best friend of over forty-five years; Michael Stierstorfer, friend and business partner; Krissi Vandenberg, standard-bearer of the "certified vegan" logo; Roy Webb, man of many talents; Pam Webb, pillar of the vegan community; Hilary Roberts, world-class copyeditor; Matthew Liebman, animal law leader; Ted Weinstein, literary guru; Shabbir Hussain, cover designer; Camilet Cooray, interior designer; and the inimitable Buddy Feldshon.

Thanks also to the interviewees for their candid and open interviews: Ori Brafman, Lex Brockington, Julie Fletcher, Syl Ko, Eve, Shelbie Murphy, Emily Norton, Jonna Paiss, and Tim Stone. Thanks also to the respondents to the online survey.

Bibliography

Books

Bentham, Jeremy. *An Introduction to the Principals of Morals and Legislation*. 1789.

Campbell, Thomas, and Colin T Campbell. *The China Study: Startling Implications for Diet, Weight Loss and Long-Term Health*. BenBella Books, 2006.

Carnegie, Dale. *How to Win Friends and Influence People*. Simon and Schuster, 1936.

Darwin, Charles. *The Descent of Man*. J. Murray, 1871.

Descartes, Renee. *Description of the Human Body*. 1647.

Descartes, Renee. *Discourse on Method,* part 5. 1936.

Donaldson, Sue, and Will Kymlicka. *Zoopolis: A Politic Theory of Animal Rights*. Oxford University Press, 2013.

Donovan, Josephine, and Carol J. Adams, editors. *The Feminist Care Tradition in Animal Ethics*. Columbia University Press, 2007.

Eiseley, Loren. *The Unexpected Universe*. Harcourt, Brace and World, 1969.

Foer, Jonathon Safran. *Eating Animals*. Penguin, 2010.

Gandhi, Mohandas. *Autobiography: The Story of My Experiments with Truth*. Public Affairs Press, 1948.

Hume, David. *A Treatise of Human Nature*. 1739; Oxford University Press, 1978.

Joy, Melanie. *Why We Love Dogs, Eat Pigs, and Wear Cows: An Introduction to Carnism*. Conari Press, 2010.

Ko, Aph, and Syl Ko. *Aphro-ism: Essays on Pop Culture, Feminism and Black Veganism from Two Sisters.* Lantern Publishing and Media, 2017.

Lappé, Francis Moore. *Diet for a Small Planet.* Ballantine Books, 1971.

Mason, Jim, and Peter Singer. *Animal Factories.* Three Rivers Press, revised, 1990.

Orwell, George. *Animal Farm.* Secker and Warburg, 1945.

Plous, Scott. *Understanding Prejudice and Discrimination.* Boston: McGraw-Hill, 2003.

Regan, Tom. *The Case for Animal Rights.* University of California Press, 1983.

Schinner, Myoko. *Artisan Vegan Cheese.* Book Publishing Co., 2012.

Scully, Matthew. *Dominion: The Power of Man, the Suffering of Animals, and the Call to Mercy.* St. Martin's Griffin, 2003.

Singer, Peter. *Animal Liberation.* HarperCollins, 1975.

Spiegel, Marjorie. *The Dreaded Comparison: Human and Animal Slavery.* Mirror Books, 1996.

Stout, Martha. *The Sociopath Next Door.* Harmony, 2006.

Stuart, Tristram. *The Bloodless Revolution: A Cultural History of Vegetarianism from 1600 to Modern Times.* W.W. Norton & Co., 2006.

Tuttle, Will. *The World Peace Diet: Eating for Spiritual Health and Social Harmony.* Lantern Books, 2004.

Wells, H.G. *The Time Machine.* William Hienemann, 1895.

Zaraska, Marta. *Meathooked: The History and Science of our 2.5-Million-Year Obsession with Meat.* Basic Books, 2016.

Articles and Reports

Allen, M. W., et al. "Values and Beliefs of Vegetarians and Omnivores." *Journal of Social Psychology* 140, no. 4 (2000): 405–22.

Bandura, Albert. "Selective Moral Disengagement in the Exercise of Moral Agency." *Journal of Moral Education* 31, no. 2 (2002): 101–19.

Bastian, Brock, and Steve Loughnan. "Resolving the Meat-Paradox: A Motivational Account of Morally Troublesome Behavior and Its Maintenance." *Personality and Social Psychology Review* 21, no. 3 (August 2017): 278–99.

Benningstad, Nora, and Jonas Kunst. "Dissociating Meat from Its Animal Origins: A Systematic Literature Review." *Appetite* 147 (2020): 104554.

Bilewicz, Michal, et al. "The Humanity of What We Eat: Conceptions of Human Uniqueness Among Vegetarians and Omnivores." *European Journal of Social Psychology* 4 (2011): 201–09.

Bratanova, Boyka, et al. "The Effect of Categorization as Food on the Perceived Moral Standing of Animals." *Appetite* 57 (2011): 193–96.

Bray, Robert W. "History of Meat Science." *The 50th Anniversary History of the Reciprocal Meat Conference (1997).*

Compassion in World Farming, *Strategic Plan 2013–2017: For Kinder, Fairing Farming Worldwide.*

Damon, W., and D. Hart. "Self-Understanding and Its Role in Social and Moral Development." In *Developmental Psychology: An Advanced Textbook*, 3rd ed., ed. M. Bornstein and M. E. Lamb (Erlbaum, 1992): 421–64.

Earle, Megan, et al. "Eating with Our Eyes (Closed:): Effects of Visually Associating Animals with Meat on Anti-vegan/vegetarian Attitudes and Meat Consumption Willingness." *Group Processes & Intergroup Relations* 22, no. 6 (2019): 818–35.

Food and Agriculture Organization of the United Nations. *Guidelines for Slaughtering, Meat Cutting and Further Processing,* 1991.

Fessler, Daniel, et al. "Meat Is Good to Taboo: Dietary Proscriptions as a Product of the Interaction of Psychological Mechanisms and Social Processes." *Journal of Cognition and Culture* 3, no. 1 (2003): 1–40.

Festinger, Leon. "Cognitive Dissonance." *Scientific American* 207, no. 4 (1962): 93–102.

Food and Agricultural Organization of the United Nations. *Tackling Climate Change Through Livestock: A Global Assessment of Emissions and Mitigation Opportunities,* 2013.

Geng, Yayuan, et al. "Oxytocin Enhancement of Emotional Empathy: Generalization Across Cultures and Effects on Amygdala Activity." *Frontiers in Neuroscience* 12, no. 512 (2018).

Grauerholz, Liz. "Cute Enough to Eat: The Transformation of Animals into Meat for Human Consumption in Commercialized Image." *Humanity & Society* 31, no. 4 (November 2007): 334–54.

Hardy, Karen, et al. "The Importance of Dietary Carbohydrate in Human Evolution." *Quarterly Review of Biology* 90, no. 3 (2015): 251–68.

Hardy, Sam, and Gustavo Carlo. "Moral Identity: What Is It, How Does It Develop, and Is It Linked to Moral Action?" *Child Development Perspectives* 5, no. 3 (2011): 212–18.

International Agency for Research on Cancer, World Health Organization. *Red Meat and Processed Meat,* IARC Monographs on the Evaluation of Carcinogenic Risks to Humans, vol. 114 (2018).

Intergovernmental Science-Policy Platform on Biodiversity and Ecosystem Services (IPBES). *The Global Assessment Report on Biodiversity and Ecosystem Services: Summary for Policymakers* (2019).

Kunst, Jonas, and Sigrid Hohle. "Meat Eaters by Dissociation: How We Present, Prepare and Talk About Meat Increases Willingness to Eat Meat by Reducing Empathy and Disgust." *Appetite* 105 (2016): 758–74.

Livestock, Environment and Development (LEAD) Initiative. *Livestock's Long Shadow: Environmental Issues and Options* (2006).

Loughnan, Steve, et al. "The Psychology of Eating Animals." *Current Directions in Psychological Science* 23, no. 2 (April 2014): 104–8.

Loughnan, Steve, et al. "The Role of Meat Consumption in the Denial of Moral Status and Mind to Meat Animals." *Appetite* 55, no. 1 (2010): 156–59.

Mayfield, L. E., et al. "Consumption of Welfare-Friendly Food Products in Great Britain, Italy and Sweden, and How It May Be Influenced by Consumer Attitudes To, and Behaviour Towards, Animal Welfare Attributes." *International Journal of Sociology of Food and Agriculture* 15, no. 3 (2007): 59–73.

McGregor, Ian, et al. "'Remembering' Dissonance: Simultaneous Accessibility of Inconsistent Cognitive Elements Moderates Epistemic Discomfort." In *Cognitive Dissonance: Progress on a Pivotal Theory in Social Psychology*, ed. E. Harmon-Jones and J. Mills, *Science Conference Series* (American Psychological Association, 1999): 325–53.

Milton, K. "A Hypothesis to Explain the Role of Meat-Eating in Human Evolution." *Evolutionary Anthropology Issues News and Reviews* 8, no. 1 (1999): 11–21.

Mitchell, Les. "Moral Disengagement and Support for Nonhuman Animal Farming." *Society & Animals* 19 (2011): 38–58.

Neal, David. "Habits — A Repeat Performance." *Current Directions in Psychological Science* 15, no. 4 (2016): 198–202.

NOAA National Centers for Environmental Information. *State of the Climate: Global Climate Report — Annual 2020.*

Norton, Carol Ann. *"Psychological Consistency, Inconsistency and Cognitive Dissonance in the Relationship Between Eating Meat and Evaluating Animals"* (PhD thesis, Institute of Social Psychology, London School of Economics and Political Science, 2009).

Orlich, Michael, et al. "Vegetarian Dietary Patterns and the Risk of Colorectal Cancers." *JAMA Internal Medicine* 175, no. 5 (May 2015): 767–76.

Orlich, Michael, and Gary Fraser. "Vegetarian Diets in the Adventist Health Study 2: A Review of Initial Published Findings." *American Journal of Clinical Nutrition* 100, no. S1 (2014): 353S–58S.

Pachauri, R. K., et al. *Climate Change 2014: Synthesis Report. Contribution of Working Groups I, II and III to the Fifth Assessment Report of the Intergovernmental Panel on Climate Change.* (IPCC, 2014): SPM 1, 1.1, and 1.2.

Pew Commission on Industrial Farm Animal Production. *Putting Meat on the Table; Industrial Farm Animal Production in America* (2008).

Pimente, David, et al. "Water Resources: Agricultural and Environmental Issues." *Bioscience* 54, no. 10 (October 2004): 909–18.

Rothgerber, Hank. "Real Men Don't Eat (Vegetable) Quiche: Masculinity and the Justification of Meat Consumption." *Psychology of Men & Masculinity* 14, no. 4 (2013): 363–75.

Ruby, Matthew, and Steven Heine. "Meat, Morals, and Masculinity." *Appetite* 56 (2010): 447–50.

Sayers, Shane. "'The Pig Who Wanted to Be Eaten': A Discussion on the Representation of Animals in Consumer Culture." *Animal People Forum*, November 24, 2017.

Scarborough, Peter, et al. "Dietary Greenhouse Gas Emissions of Meat-Eaters, Fish-Eaters, Vegetarians and Vegans in the UK." *Climatic Change* 125 (2014): 179–92.

Seigel, Emily. "Novak Djokovic Opens Vegan Restaurant, Eqvita, in Monte Carlo." *Forbeslife,* August 30, 2016.

Szeto, Y.T., et al. "Effects of a Long-Term Vegetarian Diet on Biomarkers of Antioxidant Status and Cardiovascular Disease Risk." *Nutrition* 20, no. 10 (2004): 863–66.

Tantamango-Bartley, Yessenia, et al. "Are Strict Vegetarians Protected Against Prostate Cancer?" *American Journal of Clinical Nutrition* 103, no. 1 (January 2016): 153–60.

Tantamango-Bartley, Yessenia, et al. "Vegetarian Diets and the Incidence of Cancer in a Low-Risk Population." *Cancer Epidemiology, Biomarkers, and Prevention* 22, no. 2 (February 2013): 286–94.

Testimony of Dr. James Hansen before the U.S. Senate Committee on *Energy and Natural Resources,* June 23, 1988.

Tonstad, S., et al. "Vegetarian Diets and Incidence of Diabetes in the Adventist Health Study-2." *Nutrition, Metabolism and Cardiovascular Diseases* 23, no. 4 (April 2013): 292–99.

United Nations Educational, Scientific and Cultural Organization. Executive Summary: *The United Nations World Water Development Report 2019 — Leaving No One Behind.*

U.S. Department of Defense. *National Security Implications of Climate-Related Risks and a Changing Climate,* submitted to Congress July 23, 2015.

U.S. Department of Health and Human Services and U.S. Department of Agriculture. *2015–2020 Dietary Guidelines for Americans,* 8th ed. (2015).

U.S. General Accounting Office. *Animal Agriculture: Waste Management Practices.* (1999).

U.S. National Climate Assessment, U.S. Global Change Research Program. *Overview: Climate Change Impacts in the United States* (2014).

Wang, Feiyang, and Frederic Basso. "'Animals Are Friends, Not Food': Anthropomorphism Leads to Less Favorable Attitudes Toward Meat Consumption by Inducing Feelings of Anticipatory Guilt." *Appetite* 138 (2019): 153–73.

Warrier, Varun, et al. "Genome-wide Analyses of Self-reported Empathy: Correlations with Autism, Schizophrenia, and Anorexia Nervosa." *Translational Psychiatry* 8, no. 35 (2018).

2019–2020 American Pet Products Association National Pet Owners Survey.

Videos

Andersen, Kip, and Keegan Kuhn. *Cowspiracy: The Sustainability Secret*. 2014.

"Animals and the Buddha." *YouTube*, uploaded by Dharma Voices for Animals, October 17, 2014, www.youtube.com/watch?v=S0MWAAykFuc.

"Carl Lewis on his Vegan Diet." *YouTube,* uploaded by Kinder World, May 31, 2015, www.youtube.com/watch?v=zBcyUqspQjk.

"Dr. Neal Barnard: Are Humans Designed to Eat Meat?" *Facebook,* uploaded by LIVEKINDLY, September 21, 2017, www.facebook.com/watch/?v=608156542866257.

"Dr. Neal Barnard: The Cheese Trap – Break the Addiction." *YouTube*, uploaded by Compassionate Living Events, May 11, 2017, www.youtube.com/watch?v=PHyLV3jeifk.

Kenner, Robert. *Food, Inc.* 2009.

"Official 'Glass Walls' Video by Paul McCartney." *YouTube*, uploaded by PETA, April 12, 2013, www.youtube.com/watch?v=ql8xkSYvwJs.

Psihoyos, Louie. *The Game Changers*. 2018.

"Richard Dawkins: 'I would like everybody to be a vegetarian.'" *YouTube*, uploaded by Paul Shapiro, September 29, 2013, www.youtube.com/watch?v=znMBG5DQn14.

"The Invisible Vegan Chapter 4: Stay Woke." *YouTube*, uploaded by The Invisible Vegan, February 11, 2019, www.youtube.com/watch?v=OibkuM8rh2Y.

"When Vegan Diets Don't Work #1: Dr. Klaper." *YouTube*, uploaded by Plant Based News, January 31, 2019, www.youtube.com/watch?reload=9&v=u8YlCOCEUsk&feature=emb_logo.

Index

A

animal agriculture, 27ff., 211n33
animal law, 79ff.
   Adidas, 87–89
   cause of action, 82
   Cow Palace, 86, 87, 90, 91
   dangerous dog hearings, 84, 85
   foie gras, 79, 81–83
   rodeo, 86, 90–92
   vivisection, 89, 90
   standing, 82
Animal Legal Defense Fund, 80, 92
Animal Place, 160
animal rights, 8, 19, 72, 81, 82, 123
animal welfare, 19, 81, 108, 140
animals
   as property, 64, 81, 82
   chickens, 13, 114, 142, 160
      free-range, 13, 14, 168
   cows, 12–14, 23, 113, 141–144,
      160
   fish, 13, 145
   intelligence of, 72, 138
   pigs, 12, 13, 113, 145, 160
anthropocentrism, 74, 144
anthropomorphism, 140–144
   dehumanization, 70, 141
antioxidants, 51
Aristotle, 18
avoidance, 150, 151, 158

B

Barnard, Dr. Neal, 58, 136, 178, 203
Bentham, Jeremy, 73
Blasi, Augusto, 108
Breitman, Patti, 14

B (right column)

Buddhism, 23–25, 72, 127, 132, 182,
   206
   First Precept, 23
   Mahayana, 24
   Theravada, 24
   three purities, 24, 132

C

calcium, 54
Carnegie, Dale, 15
carnism, 103
carnivorism, 178
cheese
   animal-based, 58
   vegan, 200
chickens. *See* animals
China Study, 50
cognitive dissonance, 97ff., 111ff.,
   176, 177
   in children, 123
compassion, 5, 6, 10, 11, 23, 24, 71–
   73, 77, 90, 108, 174–176, 207
   toward humans, 15, 17
convenience, 169–171, 196
   availability, 169, 171
   finances, 169, 196
   food deserts, 171
cows. *See* animals
craving, 55, 56, 59, 101, 103, 182,
   201, 203, 207
   casomorphins, 59, 203

D

Darwin, Charles, 72, 139
Dawkins, Richard, 77
Descartes, Rene, 73, 137–139
desire, 16, 56, 102, 103, 172, 174,
   207, *See also* craving

dissociation, 112, 116–118, 125
    abstract nature of, 125, 126
    categorization, 114, 115
    language, 113–115
    objectification, 113
Djokovic, Novak, 48
dying, 167

E

egg substitutes. *See* vegan food
eggs. *See* vegan food
empathy, 116, 118, 140, 174, 175, 193
environment, 27ff.
    dead zone, 42
    deforestation, 27, 29, 35, 38, 39
    extinction, 39
    global warming, 29–36, 39, 43
    greenhouse gases, 31ff.
    hunger, 29, 36–38
    land use, 36, 37
    manure, 27, 35, 42
    pollution, 27, 29, 41, 42
    resources, 28, 34, 37, 38, 44
    wastewater, 41
    water, 13, 27, 34, 38, 40ff.
    wildlife, 40
evolution, 177, 179

F

factory farms, 12, 13, 42
farmed animals
    number of, 12
feminist ethic of care, 20
Festinger, Leon, 98, 176, *See also* cognitive dissonance
fish. *See* animals
fish farms (aquaculture), 13
flavor, 101, 198
foie gras, 79, 81, 83, 168
Francione, Gary, 15, 79
free-range. *See* animals:chickens

G

Gandhi, 18, 187
Gore, Al, 31, 32

H

habit, 105–107, 146–148
health, 45ff., 204
    cancer, 50, 51
    cholestorol, 46, 50, 51, 201
    diabetes, 50, 51, 201
    heart disease, 46, 50, 53, 201
    inflammation, 51
    protein, 51, 52, 201
        amino acids, 52
    saturated fats, 51
    vitamin B-12, 53, 200
Hera, 84, 85, 86
herbivorism, 178, 179
Hinduism, 23, 25
Hume, David, 105, 139

I

In Defense of Animals, 83
insects, 4, 165, 205, 206
invisibility, 103, 125, 128

J

Jainism, 23
Joy, Melanie, 103
Judeo-Christian tradition, 21
    Bible, 21, 22, 149
    kosher, 22
    Tza'ar ba'alei Chayim, 22
judgment, 191, 192

K

kangaroos, 88
killing, 9, 10, 22, 23, 64, 71, 77, 104, 111, 117, 125ff., 149, 166–168, 180, 206, *See also* slaughterhouses

King, Dr. Martin Luther, 19, 78, 187
Klaper, Dr. Michael, 56, 103, 190, 201

L

language. *See* dissociation
Lappé, Francis Moore, 6, 52
liberation, human, 205, 207

M

Maillard reaction, 101
meat, 27, 93, 99, 101ff., 177
  as an animal, 6, 9, 61, 112ff., 195
  as cause of killing, 180
  as cause of suffering, 10, 18, 126
  as comfort food, 47, 107
  as natural, 177
  as result of killing, 9, 125, 130
  as sign of masculinity, 104
  as status symbol, 104
  craving of, 55, 56, 101
  history of, 177, 178
  in ritual, 148
  link to dairy industry, 11, 12, 18
  linked to sex, 104, 113, 157
  meat industry, 37
  organic, 14, 168
  physiology of meat-eating, 177, 178
  taste of, 101
meat substitutes. *See* vegan food
meat-paradox, 99ff., 129, 147, 151, 174, 176
meditation, 93
  metta (loving-kindness), 175
moderation, 135–137
morality, 3ff., 72, 73, 100, 108, 109, 114, 115, 125, 146, 150, 151, 159ff., 174, 177ff.
  line drawing, 162–166.
  moral disengagement, 125, 141
  moral identity, 108, 109

moral purity, 16, 162–165
Morgado, Sherry, 204

N

natural argument, 177–181
normalization, 146
norms, 77, 146, 158

O

omnivorism, 177, 179
oppression, 64–68, 74
organic. *See* meat
Ornish, Dr. Dean, 51
Orwell, George, 71

P

People for the Ethical Treatment of Animals (PETA), 11
personal responsibility, 128–134, 146
  deindividuation, 134
personality factors, 192–194
  empathy, 193
  gender, 192
  social dominance orientation, 193
  vegetarians v. omnivores, 193
Phelgye, Ven. Geshe, 127
Physicians Committee for Responsible Medicine, 58, 204
pigs. *See* animals
Plant-Based Doctors, 204
Pythagoras, 17, 18, 25
  metempsychosis, 18, 25
Pythagoreans, 17, 18

R

racism, 63–67, 69–70
rationalization, 65, 181, 182
reduction strategies, 98–100, 111ff., *See also* avoidance, dissociation, invisibility, moderation,

personal responsibility, *see*
sentience
Regan, Tom, 20, 71, 165
ritual, 148–150

S

Schwarzenegger, Arnold, 105
sentience, 20, 21, 116, 137–140
sexism, 63–67, 69–70, 76
Singer, Isaac Bashevis, 60
Singer, Peter, 19, 20, 63, 71, 114,
    122
slaughterhouses, 17, 41, 125–128
slavery, 67–69, 76
social factors, 104, 185ff.
    bonding, 187
    norms, 187
    ostracization, 188
    relationships, 188
    ridicule, 188
    socializing, 189
social justice, 171
socialization, 124
sociopaths, 109, 174
soul, 18, 25, 73
speciesism, 61ff., 140
Spiegel, Marjorie, 63, 66–69, 75
suffering, 4ff., 71, 72, 73, 77, 100,
    115, 125, 126, 131, 135–136, 139–
    140, 144, 147, 160–168, 174, 175,
    183

T

taboos, 145
taste, 101–103, 173, 198
Tryon, Thomas, 23
Tuttle, Dr. Will, 14

U

umami, 101, 198, 200

U-bomb, 101
Updike, John, 125
utilitarianism, 19, 73

V

Vandenberg, Krissi, 80
Vegan Action, i, 8, 79, 83, 155, 162
    McVegan, 8
    Reggie McVeggie, 8
    vegan logo, i, 80, 162
vegan food
    baking, 199
    beans, 201
    dairy substitutes, 199, 200
    egg substitutes, 199
    eggs, 199
    jackfruit, 198
    legumes, 52, 201
    lentils, 198
    meat substitutes, 54, 198
    nutritional yeast, 199, 200, 203
    seitan, 198
    soy-based, 198
    tempeh, 54, 198
    tofu, 54, 198, 199
vegan logo. *See* Vegan Action
Vegan Society, 18
vegetarians/vegans
    famous, 18, 36, 48, 49, 60, 75, 105
vivisection, 89, 90, 138

W

Wagman, Bruce, 80
Walker, Alice, 67, 69
Watson, Donald, 18
willpower, 106, 174

Z

Zaraska, Marta, 104, 177
Zoopolis, 21